Failure, Filth, and Fame

Joe Ranger and the Creation of a Vermont Character

Cameron Clifford

For Teddy

Contents

Introduction

This is the story of a nobody. Joe Ranger was born on a farm in West Hartford, Vermont, in 1875 and died less than three miles from his birthplace in 1964. Except for an all-too-brief period during the 1910s, it can easily be said that Joe had always lived in poverty. He worked as a farm laborer until he was thirty-six years old, briefly operated his own dairy farm, failed as a dairy farmer, and spent the last thirty-five years of his life struggling, raising calves and pigs and selling berries on his worn-out farm while also living off the goodwill of others.

So why should we consider Joe Ranger? He did nothing special. He spent his life in a provincial setting, unconcerned with the larger world outside of his own neighborhood. What could he possibly teach us?

Joe's experience is an example of how on occasion someone's reputation gets transformed by the larger forces surrounding him. In his case, those forces turned him from a poor, single, dirty, old man into a renowned Vermont character. Joe became considered special enough to be chosen for a singular part in a 1941 documentary film. He attained a cult status and was visited by scores of people who specifically sought him out. He attracted the attention of the regional media, became one of the most photographed faces in Vermont, and appeared in *Yankee* magazine two years before his death. A road is named for him. His former belongings are collected by area residents and kept as mementos and his old wood stove sits as a museum display in a local historical society.

How did all this come to pass? Joe's particularities and twentieth-century Vermont history provide the answer. Joe had a checkered background, born to a French-Canadian immigrant who relied on the public purse and part of a family considered of a different character than many in his community. Joe himself acquired a local reputation as an oddball, and after he failed at dairy farming in the 1920s, he "let himself go." He stopped bathing and gave up maintaining his property. He began regularly walking between the villages of West Hartford, North Pomfret, and Quechee, carrying a stick slung over his shoulder with a handkerchief at the end, hobo style. And while he was far from being the only local wit, he readily exhibited it in his daily encounters with his neighbors. These attributes, combined with his adoption of beaver in a pond near his house as "his own" and his claim to be able to communicate with them, created a widespread perception of Joe Ranger as different from everyone else.

Joe was also thought to be different because he never modernized. His poverty meant that he couldn't afford the new things coming into use during the 1920s and so he gave up trying to modernize his home. He lived without running water, electricity, an automobile, or central heat. His backwardness was noted as unique among those around him who acquired all the modern conveniences.

It was felt by some that Joe lived in a special world of his own not just because of his lifestyle, but because of his location. Joe's old farm was the only one left on an isolated and lonely stretch of road off the beaten path. Because of his apparent isolation, he became noted as a hermit.

But while most hermits avoid company, Joe loved having people come to visit him. Those who came expecting to find an entertaining old-timer were not disappointed, but they also found something they hadn't expected: genuine interest and conversation from Joe. He shared berries from his patch with visitors, showed them his place, talked about the beaver and other animals and plants surrounding him, and did so with enthusiasm.

Joe Ranger would have remained a local oddity had it not been for a shift in perceptions about rural Vermont and the state's success at fighting rural decline after the 1930s. When Joe was a youth, Vermont was considered a backwater by the rest of the nation. By the time he was an old man, Vermont had attained the status of a pastoral paradise. Whereas the decades before the 1930s were filled with images of Vermont and the rest of rural northern New England as decadent, in subsequent years the state emerged as a place not only to visit, but to move to.

To attract newcomers, Vermont promoted itself through images highlighting the state's rural wonders and independent Yankee farmers, and people who came sought to experience both. While getting to know the locals, many newcomers were primed to pay special attention to those they thought exhibited the typical traits of what a Yankee should be as laid out in the emerging positive popular literature about Vermont. The image of the taciturn, old, rural, independent, wit was strongly imbedded in the imagination of visitors to Vermont and they were on the lookout for prime examples. With such interest, Vermont characters became all but worshipped.

It is ironic that Joe became caught up as a central character in this fascination with Vermonters. He was in some ways the antithesis of a strong Yankee farmer. He was half French-Canadian. He had failed as a farmer. He had no achievements to be proud of.

Furthermore, his adoption of deviant ways really put him at odds with the image of the much sought after classic Vermonter. But Joe was swept up in the mania for Vermont characters anyway because the times were right for many who stood outside of the Yankee mainstream to also be looked upon as special if they exhibited the right contrary attributes. Joe was Yankee enough, what with his mother's ancestry, his years as a farmer, and his wit, but his other ways combined to make him appear unique, and that was attractive to people seeking something different than what they were accustomed to.

The celebration of Joe's special image survived him. He had been so different, that he was remembered for years after his demise. Beginning in the 1970s, as Vermont reaped the harvest of its success in attracting newcomers to the state, Joe was used nostalgically as an example of what Vermont used to be. And when contention resulted between different visions of what Vermont was to become, Joe was used as a foil against the forces of change.

Joe Ranger's identification as a special character eventually put him in a positive light during his later years, but this had not always been so. Previous to the 1930s, he was an example of a failure, and one who was a drag on rural society. His celebrity had its origins in the poverty into which he was born. We shall start our story of Joe with a view of the time and place in which the foundation of his life was laid.

1

Neighborhood

Joe Ranger was born into a Vermont farm neighborhood in 1875. His first memories revolved around the years his father, Joseph Ranger, Sr., worked on the Howard farm in Hartford, Vermont. The elder Ranger came from Canada to Vermont in the 1860s looking for work and ended up as a farm laborer for Abel Howard, and then later his son, Austin Howard.[1]

Farming in the Howards' neighborhood, where the Rangers lived, was the way of life for everyone and came from necessity and out of a long tradition. Agriculture had been the livelihood of most New Englanders since colonial times. While many had trades or special skills they employed, they all still had to farm to some extent. Population increase in southern New England during the 1700s combined with a lack of available farmland forced many to move north into what is now Maine, New Hampshire, and Vermont in order to establish new farms.[2]

The first farms established in Hartford and most Vermont towns were carved out of the forest in the years after 1760. Colonial war-

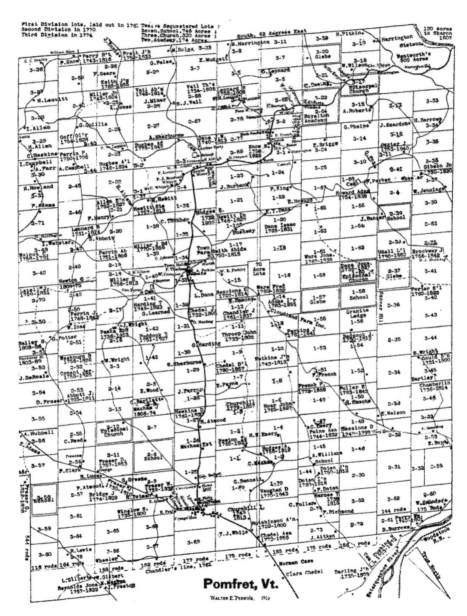

Map of Pomfret, Vermont showing original division of the town's lands in the eighteenth century. From H.H. Vail, Pomfret, Vermont.

fare with French Canada had previously stymied English expansion into the wild lands lying between Canada and the settled parts of southern New England. With peace, however, land-hungry New Englanders sought grants and settled these lands so that by 1790 almost all the land in Vermont was in the hands of private individuals.[3]

People kept coming and population increased so that by the mid 1800s Vermont was saturated with farms. The Howard's neighborhood was no exception. Hosea Doton's *1855 Atlas of Windsor County, Vermont* shows the distribution of farms in that area around the western Hartford/eastern Pomfret border region.[4]

Looking at the atlas, it is easy to find the Howard farm in the Dimmick Brook watershed. Situated a mile or so from the brook's entry into the White River, the Howards resided among a settlement of thirty-one farms stretching from the river all the way to the headwaters of Dimmick Brook in the eastern part of Pomfret.

At the time Joe Ranger, Sr. was at the Howard farm, sheep raising was the major endeavor for area farmers. While the Howards focused on raising cattle and had more cattle then any of their neighbors, almost everyone else had significantly more sheep than cattle. Area farmers also raised crops, made maple sugar, and sold pigs for additional income, but sheep and their wool was the mainstay. Chauncy Dimmick had two milk cows and two other cattle, but focused on his modest flock of twenty sheep. Further up the brook, Andrew Lamb had two milk cows and thirty sheep while William Clark kept a large flock of 150 sheep and Elisha Hazen had 180. Just over the Pomfret line, John Brockway had 180 sheep, Mrs. Udall and her son-in-law had thirty-four, and Joseph Pitkin had a small flock of ten. Up on the ridgeline overlooking the headwaters of Dimmick Brook, Alonzo Thatcher kept thirty-five sheep and across the valley Charles Kenyon had a flock of forty-eight, John Parker kept thirty-six, and three other contiguous farms had thirty-five, fifty, and fifty-seven head of sheep respectively. At the time, sheep in Pomfret outnumbered milk cows fourteen to one. The Howard's neighborhood, and Vermont agriculture overall, was oriented toward sheep.[5]

In addition to farms, the three nearby villages of Quechee, West Hartford, and North Pomfret had been established within easy reach of the Howards' neighborhood and all fit the general pattern of village creation in Vermont before the 1840s. Most villages began as mill sites. Sawmills and gristmills were vital to the growth of communities and since they needed waterpower to operate, they had to be located where there were waterfalls on a brook or a river. The Ottaquechee River, Tigertown Brook, and the aptly named Mill Brook all proved ideal locations for mills in Hartford and Pomfret. Once established by 1800, the mills naturally drew other businesses such as blacksmith and cooper shops to locate nearby. In time, resi-

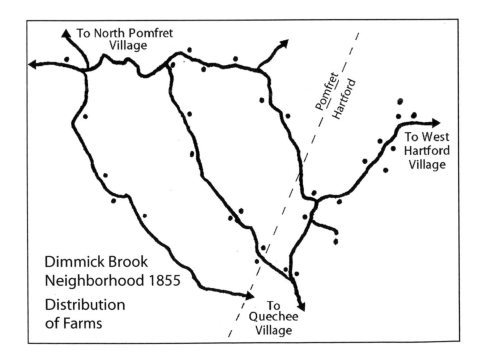

dences were built, stores erected, and public institutions such as schools, churches, and post offices established. By the 1830s all three villages in the area functioned as auxiliaries to the local farms as well as providing for the needs of the village dwellers themselves.

Over the years, technological improvements facilitated the prosperity of farms and villages. Water-powered carding machines for combing raw wool facilitated the establishment of large flocks of sheep on area farms. The replacement of old fordways with bridges, combined with upgraded roads, improved the movement of goods and people.[6]

Perhaps the most far-reaching improvement in nineteenth-century Vermont was the construction of railroads beginning in the late 1840s. The first to make its way through Vermont's valleys was an extension of a line from Boston, Massachusetts, to Concord, New Hampshire, and north to Lebanon, where it crossed the Connecticut River into Hartford, Vermont, and continued up to Bethel, passing within easy reach of those living along Dimmick Brook. The train began running between Hartford and Bethel in 1849. With railroads and rail stops every few miles, farmers found an efficient way to ship farm products and receive manufactured items from faraway cities. The future looked golden to those taking advantage of the new railroads in the 1850s.

In the long run, however, the railroads proved to be a double-edged sword to Vermont's villages and farms. Those villages located near the rail lines grew while those located up in the hills away from the railroads became obsolete. While initially benefiting all in the region, the Vermont Central Railroad proved a boon to West Hartford and a dagger in the heart of North Pomfret village. By the time Joe Ranger's father arrived in the area in the 1860s looking for work, West Hartford and North Pomfret were well on divergent courses.

Whereas West Hartford grew during the second half of the nineteenth century, North Pomfret stagnated. Without a rail stop to foster new business activity, old businesses were not replaced by new ones. A clothier's shop closed, as did the potashery, most of the small mills, and other shops. Philip Snow still operated the old Snow store and John Thurston continued with the sawmill, and a small rake "factory" was even established and in operation a few years in North Pomfret during the late 1860s. However, the factory did not survive and all business activity in the village declined. Whereas in 1850 members of the Snow family included a joiner, a shoemaker, and a carpenter, by 1870 their ranks were made up of farmers and farm laborers. Even with the decline of the Snows, no one took their place as Pomfret's business leaders. There was nothing to lead. By the end of the 1800s, North Pomfret was a sleepy little hamlet off the beaten path.

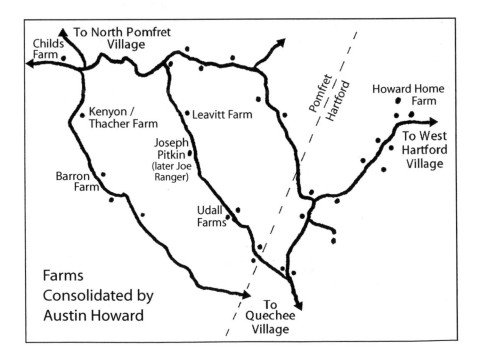

As villages were transformed by the coming of the railroad, so too were local farm neighborhoods. While initially providing a cheap way of shipping local products to the outside world, the railroad also provided a way for cheaper manufactured and agricultural goods produced elsewhere to be shipped into the area. Thus, local farmers were undercut by farmers hundreds of miles away producing the same products. With competition from farmers in the West and abroad made possible by the railroads and other improvements, sheep farming in New England became increasingly unprofitable as the decades rolled by.

It was during this era of increasing unprofitability that Joe Ranger, Sr. started a family and tried to raise his children. Local farmers struggled to adjust to the new economy and find something profitable to raise or produce on their increasingly infertile lands. While dairying had always been a part of their farm operations, it did not become dominant in the area until the 1900s.[7] By that time a number of Pomfret's hill farms had disappeared, including most of those near the headwaters of Dimmick Brook in eastern Pomfret.

The decline of Pomfret's part of the Dimmick Brook neighborhood is a prime example of what was happening locally as well as regionally to many farms throughout northern New England in the second half of the nineteenth century. Sixteen farms had persisted there up through the 1850s but were given up one by one so that by the 1910s, only five remained.[8]

The story of the Kenyon place up on the "Old Kings Highway" shows what happened to most of the farms that were given up in the neighborhood before 1910. The farm had been owned by Remington and Charles Kenyon since the 1850s, with Charles and his family occupying the farm. At some point father and son had a dispute, possibly linked to the difficulty in making the farm pay. It seems Charles wanted to leave the farm and his father wanted him to stick with it. The argument escalated so that father and son would not communicate in settling the matter. As it ended up, Remington Kenyon refused to buy his son's half interest and instead of working out the problem themselves, the issue went to court. Charles appears to have wanted to sell half of the land to someone else since his father wouldn't buy his part. The court decided that the farm could not be divided "without great loss to all parties" because there would not be enough remaining land to operate the property as a going farm. In the end, the court ruled that the whole farm be auctioned off.

Upper Left: Austin Howard, Upper Right: Ernest Howard, Below: Howard Homestead, West Hartford, Vermont. From G.A. Cheney, Glimpses of the White River Valley, Vermont....

The beneficiary of the Kenyons' misfortune was Julius Converse. Converse bought the property thinking he could make money with it. Not by farming, however. Instead, Converse planned to resell the place to another hopeful farmer. In April 1867, he sold the place to Alonzo Thacher for $1,650. Converse sold the farm expecting full well that Thacher would not be able to make a go of it. His plan was to take a mortgage from Thacher, hoping he would at least manage to farm the place a few years and pay Converse along the way. Hopefully, Thacher would eventually realize he could not make a living on the farm and have to let it go back to Converse before it was all paid for, and lose whatever money he had already paid to Converse. This is exactly what happened. Converse foreclosed on Thacher in 1876. The land was so run down by that time, however, that no one else would consider buying it as a farm. Eventually Converse was able to get rid of it in 1880 for $800. The buyer of Converse's holdings was Austin Howard.[9]

Howard's purchase of the Converse land was only one of many purchases he made in the immediate neighborhood before 1900. When someone couldn't make a go on their farm anymore, Howard bought it. Howard bought the former Ware farm Oscar Barron had up on the same ridge as the Thachers. Barron had farmed it beginning in 1864, but at the time of his death in 1882 the farm was being leased to Henry Reed, who was struggling to make a living on it. We don't know what happened to Reed, but Barron's son, Asa, washed his hands of the place, selling it to Howard that same year.

Another old farm at the end of the road to the Barron and Thacher places was also acquired by Howard. In 1883, Chauncy Childs gave up farming the place he had occupied for years, and unable to sell it to another farmer, he sold it to Austin Howard's wife, Emma. In 1894, Howard purchased another former "show farm" in the neighborhood – the Udall farm, including the Cowen place –

from Lucy (Udall) Cowan's estate. Up the road from the Udall farm, Howard also bought the Leavitt place, originally owned by one of his wife's relatives.

These and other purchases made Austin Howard master of much of the neighborhood.[10] He bought all this land not to farm himself, but as an investment. Although he integrated the Udall place into the operation of his home farm over the line in Hartford, Howard's main focus was his lumber business. He bought and logged off old wooded lots, bought standing timber, and arranged having it sawn into dimension lumber. One of his projects was supplying the lumber for the new Hartford Woolen Mill in White River Village. Although it is not known for certain, it is a pretty good guess that Austin Howard anticipated the future decline of the old hill farms. He envisioned the remaining open land reverting to forest. And, although he would never live to see lumber cut from it, he planned for it just the same. Before the land grew up to trees, Howard also attempted to make extra money like Julius Converse had by leasing the old farms to other newcomers wanting to farm. Charles Reed, probably a brother of Henry, leased the Barron place from Howard for a while, but soon gave up after failing to make any money from its depleted soil. Others also leased Howard's old hill farms, including his hired hand, Joseph Ranger, Sr.[11]

While Austin Howard was willing to invest money in consolidating old worn-out farms in his neighborhood in the 1880s and 1890s, and Joseph Ranger, Sr. was willing to try farming one of them, not many people were willing to do either. Well into the 1920s government officials, members of the press, and other leaders worried about the decline of farms in communities throughout northern New England. As conditions worsened, the public sought answers. An active media obliged, providing profiles and stories of rural communities and a people in crisis.

Popular literature in the late nineteenth and early twentieth centuries included articles about rural New England's plight and kept the image of decline such as was occurring in the Dimmick Brook neighborhood alive in readers' minds. In the 1890s the popular press ran feature stories highlighting New England's problems for a mass audience. Stories with such titles as "Decay of Rural New England" and "The Decline of Rural New England" appeared in *The Saturday Review* and *Popular Science Monthly*, along with a number appearing in the *Atlantic Monthly*.[12]

The *Atlantic Monthly* was one of the most popular magazines during the second half of the nineteenth century. Founded in Boston in 1857, it was considered by many to be the voice of intellectual America. Within its covers were published some of the most enduring negative images of New England rural life put into print. "The Problems of Rural New England: A Remote Village," "The Future of Rural New England," and "A New England Hill Town" all appeared in the *Atlantic Monthly* between 1897 and 1899.[13]

The first of this series of articles on the health of rural New England was "The Problems of Rural New England: A Remote Village." In this story about the real, but fictionally named, "Indian Ridge," author Phillip Morgan introduced his readers to the "straggling village" and its buildings "now falling into decay." After describing the village, Morgan then went on to tell of the plight of one of the town's poor who lived out of the village on a "poverty-stricken" farm. While "Nobody starves to death in our village," Morgan informed his readers, "some of the mountain folk who live far away on by-roads, in places which are often inaccessible in winter, are very poor, ill nourished and ill clothed."[14] While the article did include mention of some positive aspects of the community, the damage was done. "Indian Ridge" was decadent.

This portrait of Indian Ridge was followed in the next issue of the

Atlantic Monthly by the town of "Dickerman... in the interior of one of the New England States." Author Alvan Sanborn enumerated a whole list of ills present in this farm community. The town, he wrote, was made up of "a scattered population" among where farming "is the only industry of the people," thus keeping them poor. The roads in the community he described as "bad at all seasons." Many of the farms, Sanborn reported "have been tenantless for years" with their fields wearing "a disappointed, discouraged air." As a result, these places and many others still occupied were "gray, moss-grown, and dilapidated." Looking up at the chimneys of the houses, he saw they were "ragged" and "threaten to topple over" because they had not been maintained. The dooryards were "overgrown with rank weeds and overrun with pigs and poultry." Looking out into the barnyard he described the sheep and cattle as "lean and hungry."[15]

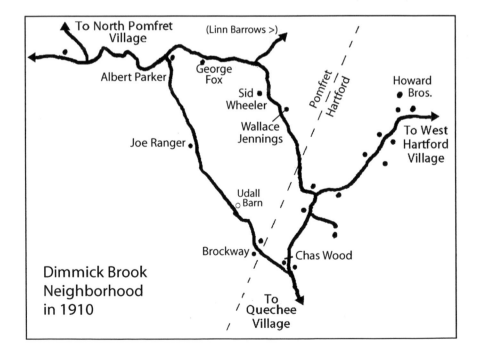

Continuing his negative portrayal, Sanborn described the local churches as "a piece with their surroundings." The schools he found to be "held in poorly equipped buildings, taught by girls without training or enthusiasm, and attended by children devoid of ambition." Of neighborliness, he wrote, "there is little." What little there is "consumes itself so entirely in the retailing of petty scandal that there is nothing left for beneficence." The civic sense of the community, he found, "manifests itself once a year only, at town meeting, chiefly in reducing the regular and necessary appropriations to the lowest possible limit, in protesting against innovations on the ground of burdensome taxes, and in quarreling over trifles." Sanborn summed up life in the town as "pinched and bare." Although he admitted that perhaps "Dickerman" was an extreme case of a community in decline, he feared that the "old New England, the New England of [profitable] farms, seem[ed] destined to disappear."16 Hyperbole, perhaps, but the message was loud and clear. Rural New England was rotting away.

Two years after Sanborn's article appeared in the *Atlantic Monthly*, Rollin Lynde Hartt penned yet another description of "A New England Hill Town" he called "Sweet Auburn." Hartt's piece focused on the degeneracy of the people. "Sweet Auburn is not a town," he reported, "it is a misfortune." Its religion "is fanciful, its morality artificial, [and] its social atmosphere morbid." The town was "like an enthusiastic invalid, joyfully making the worst of a bad matter. Instead of asserting the spirit of neighborliness, and earnestly alleviating the solitary, self-centered, insulated intensity" of their lives, the residents "shrink from one another."17

Stories such as these appearing in the late 1890s in the *Atlantic Monthly* continued to appear in print well into the 1920s as a constant reminder of the rural New England Joe Ranger's family and neighbors lived in. Journals and papers such as the *Independent, The World*

The Udall Place owned by the Howard family. Photo: Collamer Abbott.

Today, *Colliers Weekly*, and *Geographical Review* all published articles about a declining New England. A review of some of the titles appearing in these journals reveals the fixation of writers and commentators on the question of the region's health. "Broken Shadows on the New England Farm," "Is New England Decadent?," "Is New England Vanishing?," "New England's Sick Man - Agriculture," and "A Town That Has Gone Downhill" all helped to forge a negative image of New England for a generation of readers.[18]

Along with the negative images of New England farm life in general, Vermont was also specifically singled out for its rural problems. The magazine *The Vermonter* featured articles admitting to the state's decline. Although started in 1890 to help promote Vermont and improve its image, the magazine also acknowlaged the fact that no matter what was being done, the state kept losing farms, agricultural output, and population. The March, 1910 issue had an article entitled "A New Vermont," by F. Warren Wiggin, who managed the Quechee Fells Farm down the road from the Ranger's. Although the title was hopeful, it was asking a lot. After bemoaning the continued emigration from the state and the declining output of Vermont's farms, Wiggin had two recommendations for improvement. The first was for the state's farmers to focus entirely on dairying and give up the mixed farming that had been the traditional mainstay of agriculture in Vermont. The second recommendation was for the state to help by establishing "Agricultural High Schools" and introducing a course of study in agriculture in the common public schools.

Even with a dramatic shift toward dairying and increased education, the population and number of farms continued to decrease through the 1910s and 1920s. Amos Eaton wrote a piece in 1921 entitled "Vermont vs. Abandoned Farms," observing that the "number of... abandoned farms and homesteads has rapidly increased during the past five years." So much for milk cows and schools. Eaton then exclaimed to Vermont readers that because the state's farmers were "often so busy having a good time," they "are no longer improving" their lands and themselves. Therefore, he concluded, "we are not improving our communities." Didactically, Eaton told his readers that in order to succeed, Vermont's farmers "must work more and longer hours regardless of pay," adding that "Good honest hard work, intelligently directed, will accomplish wonders." The wonder is if anybody other than Eaton actually believed this.[19]

The intelligentsia certainly didn't. When writer Bernard DeVoto told his friends and colleagues in Chicago in 1927 that he was moving to New England, they were incredulous. New England was viewed as a backwater where nothing was left but the "slag of

Puritanism - gloom, envy, fear, frustration." The region was "no longer preeminent in America[n]" society. "Its economic leadership had failed..., [its] intellectual leadership had expired long ago... [its] spiritual energy...had...degraded into sheer poison," leaving the region "a province of repression, tyranny, and cowardice."[20]

Amos Eaton blamed Vermont's decline on its native farmers. Those families who were most successful sent their sons elsewhere to make a livelihood. He was concerned about who was going to take their place. "More and more," he continued, "our farms are going into the hands of less desirable citizens." Although he didn't come out and name who these undesirables were, everybody knew he was referring to degenerate Yankees, marginalized Native Americans, Irish Catholics, and, French Canadian immigrants - including among the later, the Ranger family.[21]

2

Poverty

Newcomers to rural Vermont neighborhoods, like the Howards'
Hartford/Pomfret border region, were generally welcomed by the
longer established families. Sturdy, enterprising, Yankee and northern European farm families were encouraged to join the community.
If someone thought he could come and make a living off the land, he
was welcomed.

On the other hand, those deemed of a vastly different culture
from native New Englanders, such as Catholic French Canadians,
"were not received with open arms" in rural northern New England.
This was especially true during the challenging times of agricultural
readjustment in the late 1800s, and even more so if these newcomers
were poor, like the Rangers.[1]

Joseph Ranger, Sr. was born in Quebec, and was certainly of
French-Canadian heritage. The Ranger name was common in
Quebec during the previous century. Indeed, there were thirty-two
Joseph Rangers born or married in the province between 1750 and
1765 alone.[2]

Not much else of the elder Ranger's origins is known beyond the tradition later fostered by his son in the mid-1900s that his father's mother or grandmother was a Native-American Indian.

Even though the specifics are not known about Joseph Ranger, Sr.'s move from Quebec to Vermont, they are easy to imagine. Conditions in Quebec during the 19th century became increasingly harsh for rural French Canadians as population growth and a lack of enough agricultural land to establish the upcoming generation on farms became acute. A general apathy of the Colonial Canadian government toward the plight of the rural French Canadians, combined with a lack of industrial opportunities, made life for many in the province difficult. As a result of this lack of opportunities, many French Canadians emigrated to New England.[3]

Once they got to New England, French Canadians quickly found work in urban mills. While hired as workers, they were not accepted as community members by native Yankees. In response, the French-Canadian immigrants did what many other groups coming to America did: They stuck together. In cities such as Manchester, New Hampshire, and Woonsocket, Rhode Island, French Canadians lived together in tightly unified communities, popularly known as "little Canadas." In such settings it was easy for a newcomer to fit in. He found "a social world of familiar institutions" welcoming him and encouraging him to become a part of the neighborhood.[4]

Within the town of Hartford a section of the village of Wilder, in the northeastern part of town became known as little Canada. French Canadians came to Hartford to work in its mills and by 1880 there were 279 living in town. Twenty years later the French-Canadian population was 461.[5] While most settled in villages and worked in factories, a distinct minority worked on Hartford's farms. In 1870, when Joseph Ranger, Sr. first lived at the Howard farm, he was among only twenty-two French-Canadians who chose agricultural labor out of a total of 197 living in town at the time. While the French-Canadian population in Hartford increased over the years, the number who worked on farms decreased. Indeed, by 1900 only nine worked on farms. Over the same period, those who took factory work or were day laborers in the industrialized parts of Hartford grew from twenty-four in 1870 to forty-five in 1880, to 120 in 1900. To the west, in neighboring Pomfret, even fewer French Canadians chose to settle because the town was so rural. Overall, Pomfret's French Canadians and all other foreign-born residents averaged only 2% of the town's population between 1850 and 1900, while Hartford's foreign-born population represented 14.9% of its total in 1900. Thus, the industrialized section of Hartford proved more of an attraction to new immigrants than did the rural areas around West Hartford and Pomfret. With the exception of a few, like Joseph Ranger, Sr., most immigrants who started out on farms ended up in villages and factories.[6]

Many Yankees felt that French-Canadian immigrants were a drain on Vermont. One commentator thought that "All public interests have suffered enormously by the substitution of [French Canadians] for the thrifty public-spirited [Yankee] farmers who proceeded them" in the state. Native Vermonters looked upon newcomers like Joseph Ranger, Sr. as a "shiftless, roving people" who lived "in a slipshod way." It was thought they lacked personal responsibility. Another observer wrote that "when things go well" the French-Canadian farmers and laborers scraped by, but "if sickness comes or crops short, or the winter long and hard, [they] more or less [are] dependent on the poor fund." He could have been speaking about the Rangers specifically.[7]

After initially working as Austin Howard's farmhand, and later living on another nearby farm for a while, the elder Ranger wanted to try farming on his own. An arrangement was made with Howard to lease one of the old abandoned farms Howard owned up in the Pomfret hills. At some point in the 1880s, Ranger moved his family to this farm and attempted to make a living there. His son, reminiscing years later, remembered part of his youth spent at this hill farm. The Rangers didn't stay there long, however.[8]

At some time in 1889, Joseph Ranger, Sr., became sick. We do not know the nature of his illness, but it incapacitated him. Whatever happened to the elder Ranger kept him from supporting his family for almost four years.

During this four-year period of Joseph Ranger's bout of illness and recovery the family had to depend on the town of Pomfret's poor relief system to see they were fed and clothed. Relief at that time included providing the poor with such necessities as medical attention, basic foodstuffs, everyday and seasonal clothing, educational material, soap, and even an occasional non-necessity. These items were provided either at the town poor farm or to a needy family still resident in its own household.

Pomfret Center School circa 1910. Note the two boys at front left barefoot and wearing patched clothes indicating their family's poverty. This school was where young residents of Pomfret's Poor Farm attended school. Author's collection.

Apparently, the Rangers were still trying to get by on their leased farm, or the farm of an employer, when the first relief items were delivered to them. The goods included a sack of flour, a pound of tea, a pound of soda, ten pounds of pork, 8 3/4 pounds of codfish, a bushel of potatoes, six cakes of soap, and 1/2 pound of tobacco. Before these totally ran out for the Rangers, town officials observed that Joseph would not be able to support his family in their own household for some time. A decision was made to move the Rangers to the town poor farm. The town hired John Burbank to pack up what possessions the family owned and cart them and their owners up the hill to the poor farm.[9]

The Pomfret Poor Farm the Rangers went to was the second one set up by the town. Earlier in the century the care of the poor was bid off by residents, with the lowest bidder winning the contract for maintaining the town's needy. Later, this system was given up and a farm was purchased in the west part of town so the poor could reside in one place under the supervision of an "overseer," who managed the farm and its dependents. Later, the former Smith farm located near the center of town was purchased for a new poor farm. The Smiths had been leading citizens and their home had served as a tavern and central meeting place late in the 18th century. By the late 19th century, it served as a new central place for housing the poor. This is where the Rangers came to reside in their hour of need.[10]

We get a hint of the hardening of attitudes toward the poor in Pomfret between 1880 and 1900 from verbiage used by local census enumerators in the manuscript United States Census worksheets describing those who resided at the town poor farm. In 1880 the eleven residents under the care of John Keith, the "Keeper of the Poor Farm," were listed as "Paupers," linking their current situation to economic need. In 1900, however, the five people living with "Superintendent" Lester Howard were described as "Inmates," as if they had done something wrong to deserve incarceration.[11]

We don't know how long the Rangers remained at the Pomfret Poor Farm, but the records indicate that subsequent funds were dispersed by the town for their support. Additional money was expended on schoolbooks and on a pair of boots for the "Ranger Boy." We find that at least Joe, Jr. was living "Away From the Farm" the next year. It appears the younger Ranger was working on the Royce farm in the northeast part of town when money was recorded as being spent for a "suit of clothes" for him. By the time Joe, Jr. turned fifteen years old in 1890 he was on his own, or at least away from his family, permanently.[12]

The rest of the Rangers scattered after leaving the Pomfret Poor Farm. Joseph, Sr. stayed in Pomfret and was listed as receiving money from the town in 1891 and 1892. He and his wife seem to have separated during this time. We lose track of him until 1900, when he was "boarding" with a couple, but working as a "laborer" for other neighboring farmers. Later, Ranger moved into another household in South Pomfret, and he died there of pneumonia in December 1903 at age eighty-three.[13]

Julia Ranger went to live with Gage Barrows in Hartford at some time before 1900. Mrs. Ranger appears to have done domestic work for the twenty-seven-year-old Barrows and perhaps cared for his three year old daughter while two teenage boys helped Barrows with the farm work. For a number of years Julia Ranger moved about, staying with and working for a number of different families, before moving in with her son in the 1910s.[14]

While Julia Ranger was considered "dumb" to have yoked herself to a poor, Catholic, French-Canadian agricultural worker thirty years older than herself, she did not become notorious, which was the fate of her daughter, Mary. Although considered more than dumb by many in the community, Mary Ranger may not actually have been mentally ill. Even so, she certainly exhibited undesirable traits to many through her infidelity, two failed marriages, and her inability to raise her child.

We don't know much about Mary Ranger's first husband, Sherman Daley, other than he married her in 1893. The couple most likely remained in the area, for in June 1900 Sherman Daley successfully got a divorce through the Windsor County Court as the libelant in a case of "willful desertion" against Mary. It isn't hard to understand why. At some time in the previous October, Mary became pregnant. Normally this would have been a cause for celebration, but Sherm was not the father. As it was subsequently reported on the child's birth certificate, the father of the child was one John Swanson from South Royalton, who was working as a farm laborer at the time. It is easy to envision Daley being enraged and Mary abandoning him. A month before her baby was born, Mary was living with the Maria family in Hartford, an older couple of Canadian stock who took her in. On July 8th Mary gave birth to a boy. The child was unnamed at birth and apparently given up for adoption. Little is known of him other than that he "ended up" in Washington, D.C. The details of his life are still a mystery. Mary went on to marry Marvin Unwin, but that marriage didn't last either.[15]

Mary Ranger was lucky not to have been targeted for sterilization like other women deemed problematic during the 1920s and 1930s. Vermont's sterilization program grew out of the larger "Country Life Movement," which was part of the official response to the perceived problems of rural decline and mental health. The National Country Life Movement began slowly, but gained momentum under the auspices of a Commission on Country Life appointed by President Theodore Roosevelt in 1908. After a year of research, the Commission on Country Life recommended three plans of action to fight rural decline and poverty in its final report to the president in

1909. Along with establishing the university extension system of rural education and creating a central agency to guide the nationwide campaign for rural progress, the Commission recommended that a series of scientific surveys be conducted throughout the nation to gauge the strengths and needs of specific areas, including the correlation between types of people and rural decline. As a result, Country Life surveys were conducted throughout the nation during this time by individually appointed state commissions.

Leaders of the Vermont Country Life Commission wondered whether rural decline caused degeneracy in a local native population, or if genetic degeneracy caused rural decline. A related question was whether foreign immigrants and others identified as not belonging to local communities were adding to the problems of decline and degeneracy. These questions remained unanswered, but organized state and local efforts continued to seek answers well into the 1930s and used sterilization as a research tool.[16]

Sterilization of "undesirable" people in Vermont was facilitated by the Vermont Commission of Country Life report and the efforts of its secretary, Henry F. Perkins. Perkins was the moving force for applying selective, "eugenic" principles to deal with the issues of mental health and the preservation of old Yankee genetic stock as the foundation of Vermont's population.

Perkins was professor of Zoology at the University of Vermont and was interested in researching a relationship between genetics and those deemed undesirables. Perkins believed that a link was strong. His research and reports convinced state officials that eugenics could be successfully implemented to improve the quality and character of the state's people. A successful program would also save the state – and its taxpayers – money by lowering the number of people who would need welfare, charity, or some form of institutionalization. Through a survey of families with histories of mental illness and criminal activity, lists were compiled for use in the state's efforts to break the cycle of dysfunction and dependency. Legalized sterilization by the state was instituted in 1931 and carried out among selected families.[17]

It is not known if anyone from Pomfret was ever sterilized, but it certainly happened in the area. In 2004, one Hartford resident recalled what happened to a member of a family that lived across the street from him when he was a kid in the 1920s. The whole family was considered "odd" by neighbors and throughout his childhood, he heard his parents and other adults talk about them. Looking back, he maintains that the idea of eugenics must have been prevalent because his father said that "something should be done" about one of the neighboring family's unmarried daughters who produced "retarded" offspring. As it ended up, something was done. She was eventually sterilized.[18]

Eugenic ideas were circulated in Vermont through publications. While many probably read eugenic literature in the 1920s and 1930s, they probably disposed of it after it became discredited and loudly condemned through its association with Hitler and his efforts to create a master race.[19]

However, at least one surviving copy of eugenic literature is known to have been kept by one of Joe Ranger's North Pomfret neighbors. After she died in 1994 at the age of 92, the contents of Maude Clifford's house were gone through and sorted in preparation for an auction. Clifford hadn't been interested in literature. Indeed, only a Bible, a two-volume history of Pomfret, some *Reader's Digests*, and one other book were found among her belongings.

That other book was entitled *Searchlights On Health: The Science of Eugenics* and it espoused eugenic ideas. Within its pages, readers learned the latest scientific eugenic theories put into practical everyday measures for young couples planning families, raising children,

Joe Ranger. Several copies of this photograph survive in Hartford and Pomfret, but the photographer is unknown. Courtesy of Charlotte Harvey.

and maintaining health. This copy was imprinted 1921 and was certainly presented to Clifford and her husband as a wedding present that year.[20]

While books such as *Searchlights On Health* circulated within Pomfret, familiarizing folks with eugenic ideas, the larger question remains unanswered as to the local response. Was anyone in town considered a candidate for sterilization because eugenic literature had "enlightened" a neighbor, and thus instigated action? It is easy to imagine Mary Ranger as a possible candidate for eugenic sterilization. Given her family's poverty, French-Canadian ancestry, and her own deviancy, Mary was lucky to have passed her childbearing age when the sterilization program got into full swing by the 1930s.

Along with his sister, Joe Ranger was also considered deviant by people who knew him. Voyeurism was something Joe enjoyed. Whenever he attended dances, Joe would leave before the finish and hide behind the trees at the secret lairs where departing unmarried couples would go for kissing and more, and spy on them.

Joe also practiced sexual deviancy. He engaged in bestiality. Joe had frequent encounters with a multitude of animals. Neighbor's horses, male and female, were subject to his lust, as were heifers and cows. While rarely talked about openly, some of Joe's neighbors knew that Joe "played" with animals. If his neighbors refrained from invoking the details of his encounters, Joe didn't. He wrote about them all in his diaries.

More serious in some people's eyes was the rumor that Joe was the father of his sister's child. While not true, it is telling of his reputation at the turn of the century that people believed such a thing possible of him.[21]

Even though Joe and his family avoided official identification and retribution for having the wrong ancestry, being poor, and being of questionable character, they must have been recognized as such by many in the surrounding community. If anything, the Rangers would have epitomized what was wrong with rural Vermont instead of being welcomed as an "addition" to the neighborhood. It is thus ironic that with such a history and background, Joe Ranger later became popular, even iconic, in the public imagination. Certainly, nobody could have guessed it.

3

Dairying

While the Ranger family's problems and disintegration occurred in the years before 1910, in this same period the seeds of temporary success were sown for Joe Ranger, Jr. The years between the late 1890s and the late 1920s were, perhaps, Joe Ranger's most successful. Once on his own, Joe became part of the community, worked for others, got paid, and had few expenses. Joe's neighbor, Otis Wheeler, related a story that when Joe was a young man, he worked in a sawmill in West Hartford, but more than likely Joe mainly did farm work. Laboring on a farm was what he knew best; it also was what was available for work. A look at the census records shows that the majority of single men in the West Hartford-North Pomfret area worked on farms and that Joe was one of them. In 1900 he was boarding in the home of Henry and Effie Packard in Hartford. Joe did not work for the Packards, he only rented a room from them while he worked on a neighboring farm.[1]

Very little survives from this period of Joe Ranger's life to illuminate more than a basic outline of what he was doing. However, the memory of his contemporary, Austin Howard's son Ernest, gives us a glimpse of Joe doing all right. Ernest told Ted Paronto that when Joe was a young man, he used to dress well and attended area dances. While at that point in his life, he had the time and money, and social interest, to go to dances, once he started farming on his own, Joe's dancing days were done.[2]

Joe Ranger began dairy farming after buying the former Pitkin farm near the Howards' "Udall Farm" in Pomfret in 1911. Because of the radical agricultural readjustments at the time, dairying was fast replacing sheep raising as the major farming pursuit in Vermont. Competition from the West and abroad since the 1860s had driven the price of wool down so that many Vermonters could no longer make money raising sheep. The number of sheep in Vermont steadily decreased as time went on. In 1850 Vermont had 1,014,122 sheep, by 1870 it had 580,347 and by 1900, 296,576. Farmers abandoned sheep farming as their main focus and either sold their land to neighboring farmers or tried replacing wool production with something else.[3]

Few farmers attempted to replace sheep raising with any one single endeavor, like sugaring or growing fruit. Instead, farmers did what they had always done to some extent: They hung on and pursued a number of marginally profitable avenues. Many kept their sheep, getting what they could from them while also raising cows, horses, pigs, grain, and produce, making maple sugar, and also cheese and butter from their cows.

Out of all these endeavors, dairying proved the most promising. While rural New England's population was decreasing, its urban population was increasing, creating a larger market for dairy products. The number of cheese, butter, and milk consumers had increased significantly since the 1850s. An efficient rail system linking Vermont to the rest of southern New England and New York City ensured that dairy products could be shipped and received in a timely fashion, insuring product quality and customer satisfaction.

Although cheese production was still profitable for Vermont farmers and fluid milk marketing was in its infancy, butter had become the most important farm product. In 1869, 17,884,396 pounds of butter were made on Vermont farms. Ten years later, that figure had reached 25,240,826 pounds. Production of Vermont butter grew as creameries began taking over the actual work of churning butter so that farmers could focus on producing the needed cream. In 1889, 28,399,440 pounds were made, and that figure reached 41,288,087 pounds of butter in 1899 so that by the next year, over 50% of Vermont farm income was linked to dairy production. After that, the actual pounds of butter produced in Vermont decreased, but only because its place was being taken by fluid milk as the dominant product, even as the abandonment of farms continued apace. Vermont was becoming a dairy state.[4]

In the West Hartford/North Pomfret area, dairying had been a focus for many since the 1880s. A *Gazetteer of Windsor County* from that time gives us a snapshot of the triumphant progression of dairying in the region. At the time, all of the 125 farmers of North Pomfret who advertised themselves in the *Gazetteer* could be considered "general" farmers. To some extent, they all raised small amounts of grain and produce along with livestock such as cattle, pigs, chickens, and sheep in small numbers without any special focus. While everyone who farmed was, in essence, a general farmer, those who specialized in sheep or dairying highlighted the fact.

In 1884, when the *Gazetteer* was published, sixty-five area farmers were listed solely as general farmers, with five others pursuing sugaring and fruit growing. The remaining included twenty-seven sheep farmers and seventeen dairy farmers, with eleven others listing themselves as both. One can surmise from these figures that while sheep farming was still dominant, dairying was gaining ground because those who were both sheep and dairy farmers would eventually quit raising sheep and concentrate on dairying.[5]

Essentially, the more educated, wealthier, progressive farmers were the dairy farmers while those who were less educated and not so well off were still trying to make a living producing wool. The dominant families of Pomfret, including the Hewitts, Sherburnes, Warrens, Vails, Tinkhams, Whipples, Burbanks, and Woods all were listed exclusively as dairy farmers. They had as few as Dana Burbank's six cows and as many as Stephen Hewitt's herd of twenty-five Jersey cows, with the two Sherburne families holding thirty-four, Homer Vail and Ellis Wood with fifteen each, and the rest averaging ten milk cows each. This group included descendants of Pomfret's oldest families with connections to church and town affairs, prominent newcomers with money and ambition, as well as the secretary of the Vermont State Dairymen's Association, who was also the agricultural editor of the *Green Mountain Freeman*.[6]

The Udall barn used by the Howard family for housing young cattle.
Photo: Collamer Abbott.

By the 1920s, almost everyone eventually got rid of their sheep and concentrated on dairying. In some families, dairying pushed out sheep raising through generational change. Orvis Clifford had persisted with sheep on his family's farm in North Pomfret as long as he lived. With his death in 1910, and his nephew Ed Clifford's subsequent move to the farm, sheep farming there came to an end. Right off, Ed Clifford began renovating for a herd of dairy cows. The biggest part of the project was putting on a shed addition along the entire side of the old barn for a stable where milk cows could be stanchioned side by side.[7]

While Clifford left no account of his renovations, Constance Strong wrote about the impetus for her family giving up their sheep. The Strongs lived just north of North Pomfret Village and had kept sheep in conjunction with dairy cattle for years, even though the sheep were barely earning their keep. The only times Constance mentioned sheep in her 1915 diary was when her father "shoveled manure in [the] sheep shed" and when the sheep got out through the fence.[8]

Even though the Strongs persisted with their sheep, when the younger generation was ready to take over part of the farm in 1916, the sheep were the first to go. Constance's brother, Charlie Strong, had wandered around trying to find his life's work, before deciding on farming. Eventually, he asked his parents if he could come home and farm with them. After making their decision, the elder Strongs wrote Charlie that "he could be married and come home & run the farm... and have a third of the profits." If such a plan was to succeed, however, the family needed to focus entirely on dairying. Just a few days after Charlie wrote his parents, Constance wrote that she "Helped Papa load 17 of the sheep & then went with him to the Junction with them for Mr. Baker. He got $150 for all of them (24), old Mab and a heifer." The Strongs liquidated their flock. Three days later, they

43

"Moved the calves into the sheep shed" so more milk cows could eventually be tied up in the main barn.[9]

With almost everyone giving up their sheep, it is easy to understand why Joe Ranger chose to pursue dairy farming. In addition to dairying, Joe also kept hens, raised pigs, grew potatoes, cut lumber and firewood, and worked out for others. Nevertheless, the choice of dairying as his main focus set the parameters for Joe's lifestyle. The consequence was that Joe had to follow particular daily, semi-daily, and seasonal routines connected with caring for dairy cows and their milk.

First of all, Joe had to milk his cows twice a day, morning and night. Dairy cattle produce best when they are milked between equal intervals. So, if one milked his cows at 6:00 a.m. the best time for the next milking was 6:00 p.m. Joe seems to have had two general patterns of getting up mornings. In the summer he got up at 5:00 a.m. when there was plenty of early sunlight, and in the winter it was sometimes 7:00 a.m.. and still dark when he awoke to do his "chores."[10]

After milking came "separating" the milk. Since cream was the dairy product in greatest demand farmers had to extract it from the milk. In earlier years, milk was put into pans and allowed to set until the fatty cream rose to the top. Then the farmer had to skim it off with a dipper and keep it in a cool place until enough was saved to churn into butter there on the farm. By the time Joe was dairying, centrifugal separators had been invented and were in wide use, providing an easier way for separating milk and ensuring that most of the milk's fatty content was retained.[11]

Joe made several references in his early diaries to his own separator. At one point he was buying parts for his broken separator, he later sold it and bought another one. Without a working separator, one was in trouble. There was no going back to skimming cream out of milk pans.[12]

Once separated, the cream had to be kept cool in hot weather so it wouldn't sour. This was a challenge in the days before refrigeration. Some farmers had special trunks in which they kept their cream cans cool with blocks of ice cut in the winter from specially made ponds and packed away in sawdust for summer use. Those like Joe, without ponds or coolers, resorted to keeping the cans in a shaded spring of water during hot weather. Even with these efforts many farmers in the early 20th century brought what they believed to be fit cream to the creamery only to have it declared sour and rejected, causing frustration and lost money.[13]

Along with separating and keeping cream cool came the chore of hauling it, sometimes several miles, to the local creamery. For Joe, it was a trip of over four miles to the West Hartford Creamery. Although a necessity, many farmers thought it a waste of their time to make the semi-daily trips back and forth to the creamery and had their womenfolk or children do it instead. Having neither wife nor children, Joe had to make his own trips.[14]

Ancillary to the actual handling of milk and cream were a host of other chores involved in keeping dairy cattle. First of all, of course, they had to be fed. Spring, summer, and fall found farmers planting, raising, and harvesting hay, oats, and corn for their cattle. Spring plowing came as early as the soil could be worked. Manure was hauled and spread onto fields and corn ground for fertilizer. Corn was planted and oats were sown. As the corn grew, it had to be kept weed free either by hand with a hoe, or with a horse-drawn cultivator. Once July came, grass was mowed, tumbled, dried, and hauled to the barn to be stowed away as hay for winter feed. Haying continued for much of the summer for many, depending on how much was needed. Come fall, for those who had silos, corn was cut and carted to the silo where it was chopped with a mechanical chopper and put into the silo as "ensilage feed." When spring came, the cows were let out during the day to forage on the new green grass growing in the pastures.

Farmers raised corn, grass, and hay, but they also needed to purchase products to feed to their cattle. Supplements such as salt and other minerals had to be bought and made available for cattle to maintain their health. In addition, ready-mixed dairy grain had to be bought and fed out so the cows would be able to produce the maximum amount of milk possible. Cows thrived on the supplemental grain, and produced more milk on it, but it was expensive and required additional hauling and handling for the farmer.[15]

Examining Joe's diaries, it is apparent that in his early years of farming he kept on top of providing for his cattle. Providing cows with green grass in the pasture and hay in the barn along with plenty of water was the bare minimum if a farmer expected his animals to live. Anything beyond that depended upon how much money and time one wanted to invest in the stock. Joe provided his cows with plenty of grain. In 1918, Joe reported that he "payd out" for grain thirty-two times. Although he rarely wrote down how much grain he picked up at a time, on July 12, 1918, he noted that he had picked up 400 lbs. and then another 400 lbs. on the 31st. While we don't know for sure how many cows he was milking at that time, it probably was between three and six.[16]

Instead of trying to estimate a ratio of pounds of grain per cow he fed, it may be helpful to understand Joe's commitment to keeping his cows well fed if we compare the amount of money he spent on grain in relation to the amount he received for his cream. During 1919, Joe spent a total of $543.89 on grain and received $823.62 from the West Hartford Creamery for his cream. Providing grain to his cows took 62% of his cream money. Joe Ranger fed his cows well, but he got little in return. He was only subsisting.[17]

Interdependency was an integral aspect of dairy farming. The image of farmers willingly helping each other with the seasonal rounds of haying, cutting corn, and cutting wood along with helping in times of need is one many associate with nineteenth- and early-twentieth-century farming in Northern New England. While farmers indeed worked together, the world of mutual help was complicated, and sometimes unfair.

One of the complications of Joe's farming life was that he had no family to help him, unlike almost everyone else in the area. Without a wife or children, the round of chores took longer than if he had help. The one activity that did not take long was the housework: Joe simply didn't do any. The farm work, however, took much of his time, and whenever he needed assistance he had to depend on his neighbors.

Joe's dependence on his neighbors for help was natural enough. To some extent, everyone depended on someone else in Vermont's rural neighborhoods to help out with large seasonal chores, to fill in when someone was sick, or as steady hired help.

Sometimes Joe had problems dealing with his neighbors, though - especially when they owed him money. Linn Barrows had owed Joe money for some time when Joe confronted him about the fact late in January 1920. Their talk was not amicable. Joe described it as a "tung lashing" with Linn telling Joe he would pay him when he was good and ready and Joe threatening that maybe Linn "would pay me before if he did not look out." It was an idle threat. Later in March, Joe lamented "I gess he will always ou me." Barrows did make a token payment of .07 cents in April but the issue was evidently still unresolved in August when Joe noted that he'd spoken with Ralph Barrows earlier in the day about Linn and lies.[18]

Linn Barrows was not the only one in the neighborhood who owed Joe. When Joe sold potatoes to a fellow at the West Hartford Creamery, he noted that they hadn't been paid for. Also unpaid was the hay George Fox got from Joe's barn in April when Fox was almost out of hay at his place. Joe knew he would eventually get his money from these folks, but he had to keep close track of who owed him what.[19]

When he felt wronged, about money or work owed him, Joe wrote about it. In January 1918 he tried to get Henry Brockway's son, Dan, to "come up" to give him a hand, but he "says he don't wont to." Two days later, however, Joe was down helping with Dan's chores. On February 25, 1920, when Joe expected Charlie Wood to help him saw firewood, it didn't turn out that way. Joe wrote with bitterness that Wood had "come up to day but did not saw wood he went rite back home." Joe sawed by himself.[20]

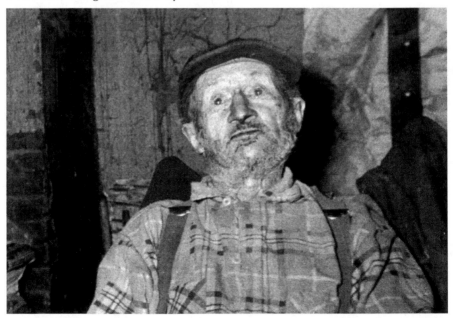

Joe Ranger inside his house. Photo: Wayne Thompson.

Even though Joe felt slighted, he still continued to work for both Dan Brockway and Charles Wood because he needed the money. Indeed, Joe worked extensively for his neighbors, while at the same time maintaining his own farm. The work Joe did for his neighbors included big jobs such as haying, filling silo, and cutting firewood. This work had to be done every year by everyone and required multiple days to complete. Depending upon the size of the farm, haying took up many days of the summer. While silo filling did not take as much time, it involved cutting corn, hauling it to the silo, and unloading it into the chopper. Cutting firewood took weeks, but it was one of those activities saved for times of little other work, usually during the winter.[21]

Annually, Joe took on a combination of plowing and harrowing, haying, silo filling, and getting up firewood for his neighbors. Some years he did more of one kind of work than another, such as cutting wood for several people but not cutting corn, or haying but not filling silo. However, from his earliest diaries and continuing throughout his active farming years, Joe Ranger was always working for his neighbors on some long-term farm chore.[22]

The first we know of Joe Ranger working for a neighbor on a long seasonal job while trying to get by on his own farm is in 1918. Joe's diary opens with him chopping and cutting firewood for Ernest Howard up on the Howards' land "over her in the woods" near Joe's on January 22nd. Joe put in eight hours that day and over the following three days he put in less each day, diminishing to only four hours on the 25th after Joe had come back from taking his cream to the creamery. This is no indication of a declining interest or laziness on Joe's part, just adaptability. He made the job fit his schedule since there was not a specific rush to finish it. Besides, other times he worked more.[23]

Indeed, that Saturday, January 26th, Joe chopped wood eight hours. After taking off Sunday and Monday, he chopped Tuesday afternoon four hours and kept up his pace of alternating long and short days chopping for Ernest Howard over the next several weeks. Sometimes he indicated clearly in his diary why he didn't chop on a particular day. Sundays he "staid at home" and didn't work. Other days, however, he either did his own "work and chores" instead of chopping, or he went after grain or groceries. One time he noted that he had bought a new pair of mittens in the morning and then apparently wore them in the afternoon to protect his fingers from the cold while chopping for three hours. On February 19th he only worked two and a half hours chopping in the morning and then "ground [the] axes in the afternoon." By March 2, he was splitting the firewood "with the machine." Once the splitting started, Joe only worked four more days. On March 13th, he wrote that he worked for Ernest seven hours and "finished up to day." In all, Joe had worked a total of 133 1/2 hours on the Howards' wood that winter and spring.[24]

The other long-term job Joe did for a neighbor in 1918 came right on the heels of finishing up chopping for Ernest Howard. Eleven days after Joe got done with the Howards' wood, Albert Parker came over to see him. Joe wrote that "we went up to" Parker's "to see about sugaring." As with the Howards, Joe worked a few hours some days and more others, depending on the sap run. Evidently Joe helped Parker tap the first two days and then commenced gathering sap beginning on March 28th. For three weeks Joe went up to Parker's and helped gather eleven different times. It seems that the sap ran well, and perhaps they finished tapping the trees on the 29th and 30th, as Joe worked six hours each of those days. After that it seems the average round of gathering sap, including hitching up the horses to the sap sled, gathering all the buckets, and emptying the load at the sugarhouse, took three hours. Joe doesn't mention if Albert helped with the gathering. Parker most certainly did all the boiling of the sap into syrup. By April 16th, the season was over and Joe put in seven hours gathering the last of the sap and taking down the buckets and pulling the spouts from the trees.[25]

The next year Joe helped Albert with haying. On July 7th, after going to the creamery that morning, Joe "worked 3 ours for parker haying." For six days straight, Joe hayed for Albert. Three of the days he worked eight hours, one day seven hours, one day six hours, and the three hours on the first day. During this stretch, Joe brought his own horse four days to help pull Albert's hay rake and hay wagon. Sunday the 13th Joe did not work, but he started in again on Monday after getting back from the creamery. On Tuesday Joe noted that he and Albert "settled to date" and found that Albert "ous me 40 ours."[26]

That did not end Joe's haying for Albert. Joe began haying his own place on the 15th of July and stopped on the 19th to go back to helping Albert with what was unfinished at his place. From the 21st to the 29th Joe worked every day except Sunday the 27th, helping Albert. He put in thirty-nine hours that week for Parker and then went back again to doing his own haying.[27]

In 1920, Joe hayed for Albert Parker again. There was a twist, however. In January and February, Joe helped Albert load hay from Parker's barn onto a sled fourteen different days so Parker could sell and deliver it in Quechee. Along with this special winter haying, Joe also helped Albert twelve days during the regular haying season in July and August. Not only did Joe work with Parker on hay that year, he also cut wood seven days for Albert.[28]

After giving Parker a hand in August, Joe began thrashing oats at Dan Brockway's farm and continued into September. Also in September, Joe commenced cutting corn and firewood for Charlie

Wood. Once they were finished, the big seasonal jobs Joe tradition-
ally did for his neighbors ended for that year.[29]

Seasonal work continued the next year, however. In 1921, Joe
expanded the seasonal work he did for his neighbors, most likely
because of a dire financial situation he was facing at the time. That
year began with him cutting wood for John Brockway, Charles Wood,
the Pratts, and George Tenney. He didn't do any haying for anybody
that summer, but come August he was busy thrashing oats for his
neighbors. No sooner did he finish thrashing on August 27th, he
started in cutting corn and filling silo on the 29th. For thirteen days
Joe cut, hauled, and chopped corn, ending on September 20th.[30]

While Joe worked extensively for his neighbors, they also helped
him on the occasions when he needed it. The Jennings helped Joe
plant his corn in 1918 and George Fox did the same the next year and
also assisted Joe with his potatoes. After Joe had finished haying for
Albert Parker in July 1919, he got his own haying done with the assistance of "2 men and one boy," apparently Parker among them. Later
that summer Sid Wheeler helped Joe thrash his oats and then come
winter Albert Parker worked for Joe drawing out logs and peeling
pulp.[31]

Joe Ranger didn't trade work with his neighbors that often. He
used their assistance sparingly, and instead, worked for them for cash
whenever possible. Because his own dairy operation was growing
increasingly unprofitable, as we shall see, he needed the money.

4

Failure

During the 1920s, Joe Ranger faced two crises. The first was trying to pay for the care of his mother. Area residents who remember Joe claim that his mother used to live with him off and on over the years. Indeed, some have vivid memories of her at Joe's house. Otis Wheeler's brother, Burton, first remembers seeing Mrs. Ranger and knowing who she was when he spied her one day washing clothes down in the brook by Joe's house with a clay pipe in her mouth. Naturally the two things that struck Wheeler as a child were that this woman did her laundry in the brook and she smoked a pipe.[1]

An equally impressive picture was stamped in the memory of Ernest Howard's son, Walt, as a child. One day Walt and his sister, Pauline, rode over to Joe's with their father's brother, Ralph, who had to talk to Joe about some work he wanted done. As Ralph and Joe stood visiting in the barn, Walt and Pauline walked around the barn-yard exploring. They went over to the house and decided to peek in the door to see what sorts of things Joe had inside. To their surprise they saw an old woman with a shawl draped around her, sitting in a rocking chair, smoking a pipe. She saw the children and, grinning, leaned forward and told them, "I'm Joey's mother." First surprised, and then scared, Walt and Pauline turned and scooted right back to Ralph. Walt remembered that as the only time he ever saw Joe's mother.[2] Others also remember that Mrs. Ranger sometimes lived with Joe, sometimes with daughter Mary, and sometimes elsewhere, such as the Pomfret Poor Farm.

The first mention Joe made of his mother in his diaries was on January 23, 1919. Mrs. Ranger was living somewhere else, either with Joe's sister or in a household where she worked. At the time, however, she was in no condition to work. She was not well and wrote her son asking if she could "come back" and live with him, as she evidently had before. Two days later she wrote again. With Joe's consent, she arrived "Just at night" on the 31st. She must have been driven there in a buggy, because "she could not walk." Over the following couple weeks, Joe attempted to both take care of his mother and get his chores done. It appears her condition did not improve, however. On February 18th, Joe walked down to Dan Brockways to use

North Pomfret Village circa 1910. Collection of the author.

their telephone to call the doctor to come see his mother.[3]

What the doctor found when he got to Joe's is a mystery. However, while we don't know the nature of Mrs. Ranger's ailment, or what the doctor prescribed, it was clear that Joe couldn't care for her. Arrangements were made and sometime that month she moved again. Her destination: again to the Pomfret Poor Farm. The Pomfret Town Report listing income and expenses for 1919 shows an entry for $2.00 received from Joseph Ranger for "expenses of moving mother to [poor] farm."[4]

Since the Ranger family's last stay at the Poor Farm almost thirty years earlier, attitudes toward the poor had not improved. In part this was because of a popular perception, thanks to eugenic research, of a link between poverty and genetics. In addition continued population loss left even fewer people to support the poor than in the previous century, ensuring that resentment toward those relying on public welfare remained high.[5]

While the Rangers had lived at the poor farm years ago, the fact that Julia Ranger ended up there again was particularly humiliating to Joe. He had worked himself out of the poverty of his youth, bought his own farm, and thought he could face whatever challenges came his way. The fact that he couldn't care for his mother when she now needed him, was especially galling. The thought that he had failed his mother worked on Ranger, depressing his spirits and interfering with his daily work. On February 25, 1920, Joe unhappily recalled the event that led to his mother's decline and present situation at the town farm. It was "just 2 years ago to day mother went away down to Claremont new hampshire." She had "sayd she was happy and everything was nice" but "she lied about it to me."[6] At the one-year anniversary of his mother moving to the Pomfret Poor Farm, Joe wrote in his diary that "one year ago I was happy[,] look at me now."[7]

Joe was not alone in feeling responsible for his mother. Naturally, Pomfret town officials did also. The care of the destitute was still a town function. However, if the poor person had family members in the area, the responsibility for care fell on the kin. Even if the family was unable to administer care directly, and the sick person had to be cared for at the poor farm, the kin were held liable for the cost of care. Thus, those who didn't have family were cared for by the town for free, and those with family had their cost of care charged back to the family by the town.[8]

No doubt, Joe expected to be held liable for his mother's care and even though he knew it, and couldn't afford to pay, he had little other choice than to have the town take her in. She needed help.

At the time, Joe had no way of reimbursing the town for his mother's care. After she had been at the poor farm almost a year, Joe noted on January 30, 1920, that he had taken in $66.06 so far that year and paid out $67.67, in the red for $1.61. Joe's financial situation did not improve. By the end of February his expenses were $28.58 more than his income and he was still in debt in March. He did manage to pay "the docter 3.00 for mother['s care] last spring," adding that the doctor had "waited almost one year" for his fee.[9]

Things got worse for Joe, however. April 5th he ran "out of grain for my cows for the first time" because he didn't have the money to buy any. Things were getting desperate and on the 9th, when he went to the creamery with his cream he made two deals in the village, selling six of his cows. Joe sold four cows to "mrs hazen" of West Hartford. The other two cows he sold while at the creamery to someone from Sharon who was there delivering his own cream. Joe got a downpayment of $15.00 on them and agreed to deliver them to the farmer the next week. Early the next Friday morning Joe and one of his neighbors led "dina and sara" down the hill and "up to sharon." Selling these two old cows bothered Joe, since he had probably raised them up from calves and owned them for years. Later that evening, Joe lamented that he "hated to see sara go." He then let loose his frustration, claiming that he had to sell her "just on account of an old fuck stick," referring to one of his creditors.[10]

After spending the next day at home by himself burning brush, Joe cooled down a bit. He looked back and figured that whereas at the same time last year he had "10 hed of cattle – to day I hant got only 6 hed." While Joe may have had six cattle when he wrote on April 18th, the next day he had only five. Figuring his accounts, he still didn't have enough money to satisfy those he owed, so he sold another cow. This one went to Dana Murgatory and Joe, numbed by now, noted the deal matter of factly.[11]

With this final sale, Joe then had enough money to go down to the "Junction" in Hartford and pay off $198.75 he owed to Mertie Howard, the aforesaid "fuck stick." Howard was the wife of Frank Howard (again, another Howard unrelated to the others), from whom Joe had bought his farm and originally mortgaged the place to. Back in 1914, Joe was in need of cash and approached the Howards about refinancing the farm. Mertie Howard then took a new mortgage and lent Joe $246.87, enough to pay off the old mortgage to Frank and give Joe the extra money he needed. This second mortgage differed than the original one, however. Mertie Howard was greedier than her husband, and structured this second mortgage so that she could make all she could off of Joe. The mortgage specified no set date when Joe had to pay back the loan. Instead, the document simply stated that the money was due "on demand," meaning whenever Howard asked for it. Since she was to receive 5% interest on the money owed, it was in her favor to encourage Joe not to worry about paying off the principal amount he owed her. She would have a steady income from the interest money, and Joe could easily pay the small annual interest amount without having to worry about the larger amount he owed. While seemingly beneficial to both parties, this sort of loan was weighted in favor of Howard because she could ask for the whole of the principal on demand, requiring Joe to either pay up or turn the place over to her, minus all the interest money already paid.[12]

The biggest problem with the mortgage for Joe was that he was dependent upon Mertie Howard's whim. She could make him pay the total amount owed any time she wanted. After six years of milking Joe for what she could, in the spring of 1920 she apparently heard Joe was having money troubles and decided to ask for her money. It would be charitable to Howard to assume that she called in the loan from Joe at this time because she feared he might go broke, leaving her with a legal mess. However, more than likely she did so thinking he wouldn't be able to raise the money and have to turn over the farm to her. Thus she would have gained six years' interest, and Joe's farm to resell. It didn't work out that way, however.

By scrambling, selling his cows, and getting together what money he could, Joe Ranger managed to pay off Howard and get out of her grasp. But the price was high getting free of Mertie Howard. For about a year he didn't have enough milk to make it worthwhile to separate the cream and sell it to the creamery. On May 17, Joe wrote that he had gone to the creamery that day "for the last time for a long time to come" until some of his young stock would calve and produce milk.[13] During this time Joe worked for his neighbors and tried building up his stock by buying heifer calves that would be able to give milk in a couple of years.[14] He was discouraged, however. On July 4, 1920, while others were celebrating Independence Day, Joe came back from cultivating John Dana's potatoes and felt especially downtrodden. He compared his present situation with his "happy" one in the past and concluded: "look at me to day got nothing but shit."[15]

As a result of Joe's money problems in 1919-1920, it appears he paid nothing to the town toward his mother's bill. No doubt, the Pomfret selectmen came over to talk with Joe about it, but they always left without any money. No one particularly wanted to oppress Joe, but he owed the town money and he had to pay up. Town officials finally acted on April 21, 1921. That day, Joe wrote, "the town [at]tached my stock for mothers bord to day."[16] They put a lien against his animals so that if he sold any of them, the money had to go to the town instead of his own pocket. At the same time the town turned to a lawyer for help. The lawyer promptly began a legal action against Joe.

The suit got Joe's attention. As we have seen, Joe was in dire financial straits at this time, but he thought he might be able to offer the town $2.00 a week for his mother's care and board. Attorney Loren Pierce of Woodstock represented the town in the suit and responded on May 19th to Joe's proposal. While Pierce didn't reject Joe's offer, he countered in his letter that "if you will pay $3.00 per week and the costs to date" associated with the suit, the town "will accept same in full settlement of the suit." Pierce then enumerated that Joe's mother "has been boarded 83 weeks which would amount to $249.00, and the costs" making "$264.00." A mouse has chewed a section of Pierce's letter, destroying much of the last paragraph, but the words "Please advise me at once!" are still legible.[17] It seems that Joe responded that he had no money, but would work off what he could for the town by working on the roads that year as he could.

This proposal evidently was accepted and Joe began on June 7th, working ten hours that day "on the road beyond the Cowen place." The next day he put in another ten hours and then on the 10th he put in sixteen hours on "the road up to foxes and over to the Cowen place." On the 11th he worked ten hours by the Fox place. He had put in forty-six hours of work amounting to $13.80 credit against his mother's account.[18]

After haying that summer, he started in again working for the town on August 2. For six days, Joe cut brush beside the road and picked stone out of the right-of-way. That September he spent several days over to the town farm helping fill silo, apparently getting credit. Joe stopped working for the Town of Pomfret on September 11th and did not do any other work for the town that year. Since there are no extant diaries for the rest of the 1920s, we can't tell if Joe commenced working for the town again the next year.[19]

It is easy to imagine that with his cattle coming back into their milk and his own work taking up much of his time, it was unlikely that Joe worked any more for the town. Although this is pure speculation, one surviving piece of paper in the Pomfret Town Clerk's office indicates its likelihood. On January 25, 1922, the town accepted a sort of mortgage deed from Joe Ranger for $345.00. Although not stating explicitly why this mortgage was executed and what the money went for, at that time Joe's mother had been boarded by the town for 121 weeks, equaling $363.00. Joe had worked off around $30.00 of the bill, leaving a balance of $333.00, and if we add in the legal costs, which certainly were charged against Joe, the total would have been around $345.00.[20]

Joe Ranger tied his place to a mortgage again in order to pay off his mother's bill for care at the Pomfret Town farm. We shall see later on the role this mortgage played in deciding the fate of Joe's property, but for the time being the town was content with the mortgage from Joe. The town was satisfied and Joe probably took his mother back home. We don't know the state of her health at the time, or how much she stayed with Joe over the next fourteen years, but this indeed was around the time Walt Howard got his one and only peek at Joe's mother. At any rate, the town's suit against Joe was settled. Julia Ranger alternated living with Joe, his sister Mary, and others over the years until her death on March 21, 1936.

Although Joe was able to care for his mother some of the time over her remaining years, her obituary in the *Vermont Standard* stated that her death was "at the home of Robert Gilmore, where she was being cared for." At the time, Gilmore was Pomfret's overseer of the poor. In his mother's final hours, Joe had failed her again.[21]

In part, Joe's financial problems stemmed from the farm itself. He had purchased it because it was cheap, and it was cheap because it was worn out. So, Joe started out at a disadvantage right from the beginning. Because of his financial crisis and inability to make a profit on his farm in the early 1920s, Joe was unable to keep up and adapt to the subsequent changes that were becoming required for producing, preserving, and transporting dairy products, or adopting any other improvements.

During the 1920s rapid change transformed dairying in rural Vermont. Village creameries gave way to direct shipment of cream and milk to Boston's milk plants. Trucks replaced horses in transporting dairy products to railroad transit points, and then replaced rail for shipping milk directly to the processing plants. Electricity brought light and new equipment into the farmer's home and barn. Improvements in cooling cream and milk developed. Concern for cleanliness and production became paramount. It was an exciting time of change.[22]

Constance Strong left behind one of the best accounts of farm improvement years after she had documented her family's sale of their sheep. She subsequently married her neighbor, Elton Clifford and in 1928 she enumerated the changes they were making on their North Pomfret farm. Among them was the instillation of a "new" engine and pump for the milking machine in the barn and new hot water pipes for the house. The couple already owned a car and had a telephone. A "doctor" came to test the herd for tuberculosis. Elton bought life insurance so that if anything happened to him, Constance would be provided for. Improvements were made in the kitchen, with a new cabinet that was "gray enamel with white porcelain top [and] Has compartment[s] for flour, sugar, [a] bread box, glass containers, [it was] Great!"[23] Constance also was able to buy a new Maytag washing machine and after using it concluded that there was nothing like it: she got the laundry done and on the clothesline in 1 1/2 hours. The couple hired help for the house and farm and in June they were having a "milkhouse" built with a tank for keeping the cream and milk cool.

Labor-saving devices such as the milking machine and clothes washer freed up time for other important chores. The milking machine made milking easier and quicker. After finishing the milking, Elton was able to start something else, while Constance was able to get "the milk things" cleaned and ready for the next use, in part because of these labor saving devices like the washing machine. New machines didn't necessarily "save" time, but rather, redirected saved time to another chore. Constance was also able to run errands, such as bringing the horses to West Hartford to be shod, relieving Elton from that job.[24]

While it seems like 1928 was a year of change for the Cliffords they, and most other families, slowly adapted to new technologies and expanded their dairying activities accordingly. It was 1930 before the Warrens, also a North Pomfret family, got electricity on their farm along with an oil kitchen stove "which works beautifully [with e]ven heat."[25] Mary Warren also noted other kitchen improvements the family had made, along with the purchase of an automobile, which "We needed very much indeed."[26]

Unlike the Cliffords and Warrens, Joe Ranger did not document improvements on his farm. There was nothing to write about. In fact, far from improving, by the late 1920s his farm had deteriorated to the point that he wasn't shipping cream or milk at all.[27]

Joe had to give up shipping cream because he could not invest in the improvements he needed to make in order to ship dairy products. When the West Hartford Creamery went out, farmers shipped their cream out of the region for processing. With this change, keeping the cream, and also milk, from souring became more of a concern than previously. Before, once the cream came to the local creamery it was immediately processed, but now it had to travel an additional hundred and something miles to the Boston processor. Cutting down on bacteria in the milk and keeping it cooler were two things farmers accomplished by investing in enclosed milking machines and improved coolers, including electric models.[28]

There was no way Joe could invest in this new equipment. First of all, his farm was too small to make buying a milking machine and cooler feasible. Second, he didn't have the money to purchase more land to support an expanded herd, or get credit to do so, as others did.

Not only did Joe not get new equipment, he still didn't have the basics most had acquired by the late 1930s. He had no running water other than what ran by his house in the brook. There was a spot where the brook ran under the road through a culvert where he dipped out whatever water he needed. He had no electricity. Like other remote farms, Joe's was too far away from the power lines to make it cost effective to run the wires to his place. Joe never bought an automobile, nor learned to drive. It even got to the point where he no longer had a team, just a single old horse. Naturally, he had no tractor. As opposed to his neighbor's expanding herds, Joe had fewer cattle than in previous years.

Even though Joe had to stop shipping cream, he still got by milking cows. For a short time after the processors wanted fluid milk instead of cream, Joe hauled his milk to the end of his road where the truck picked it up along with the neighbor's milk. For a while after he no longer had a team of horses to haul the milk out with, he resorted to lugging it out himself with a neck yoke. He soon gave that up, however.[29] At that point, even Joe had to admit he had failed as a dairy farmer.

Joe Ranger outside his house. Photograph probably taken by Seymour Hazen. Photo courtesy of Betty Cross.

5

Readjustment

The result of Joe's failure as a dairy farmer was that sometimes he had to beg and steal in order to get by. Numerous people in the area fed him, sometimes when they hadn't expected to. In the 1930s, when Ted Paronto worked for Ralph and Ernest Howard after they had jointly taken over their father's farm, Ted was living in the hired man's house down the road from the main house, and he had got to know Joe. One Friday as Joe was walking by Paronto's home, he spied Ted out on the porch so he stopped to visit. While they were talking, Ted's wife called from inside the house that dinner was ready. Ted asked Joe to "come in and have some dinner" and Joe did. He evidently liked what he had, for after that, Ted said, every Friday at dinner time Joe Ranger would show up to eat.[1]

Joe not only took advantage of offers for food, he also helped himself when no offer was forthcoming. The Howards were one family Joe stole from. Their orchard was near Joe's and too handy to ignore. Since Austin Howard first purchased the Udall place, the family had improved the old apple orchard and planted new trees as well. Ralph Howard was mainly concerned with its care, and the results were admirable. The family was known for their apples and shipped them far and wide. So much effort and focus was put on the apples by Ralph that his nephew John tired of dealing with the orchard. Because of the hours he spent with apples during his youth, John Howard was later heard to proclaim that the "best way to prune an apple tree is right tight to the ground."[2]

Joe had his own apple trees, so he did not take any of the Howards' apples. However, he did help himself to the other fruit growing in the orchard. Ted Paronto's son, Tom, remembers going to the Udall orchard with the Howards to pick apples when he was a kid in the late 1930s and specifically recalls one plum tree by the end of a stone wall that had beautiful fruit. When the fruit was dead ripe, it was delicious. It was rare, however, that Tom, or the Howards, got to the plums before someone else. That someone was Joe Ranger. Joe was as timely in getting the plums as a racoon getting ripe corn before the gardener. Tom doesn't remember the Howards making an issue over it, but they knew what was going on.[3]

Plums were not the only crop of the Howards Joe helped himself to. Ernest and Ralph wintered their young cattle in the old Udall barn and for some years paid Otis Wheeler to care for them. Joe had always had enough hay to feed his own animals, but one spring he ran out. Joe must have been in his seventies and keeping one cow when Otis observed a daily phenomena. When Otis got to the barn in the morning, he noticed tracks heading in and out with scatterings of hay spears on the snow. Someone was taking hay and further investigation showed that the person was taking it to Joe Ranger's place. Joe would come early in the morning with a large beet pulp bag, fill it with hay, and carry it back home for his cow. Otis recalled years later, "I never said nothing about it [to] Ernest cause they had plenty of hay."[4] In Joe's eyes, the Howards had enough of everything, so they could afford to lose some of what they had to him.

Joe Ranger didn't live exclusively off his neighbors during his later years. He continued to raise animals. Instead of selling the milk from his dairy cows, he fed it to pigs and calves, raising them up and later selling them. In this way, he efficiently made use of the milk his cows gave, with little bother, even if he didn't make much money at it. His diaries for the late 1930s have numerous entries mentioning his cows and calves. In June 1937, Joe wrote that one of his cows had a calf, without indicating which cow, or the sex of the calf. The following March, "Saria" calved. In April, when he turned his cattle out to pasture, he had three cows and "4 hed of young cattle."[5]

Joe kept close track of his cow's breeding cycles in anticipation of calves being born. On May 21, 1938, he noted that "Topsy was in heat" and two days later that "floria went to Bull." In the spring of 1944 Joe was busy watching his cows get bred. He mentioned "dina," who was bred March 2nd and "will calve dec 9", and "cara [who] will calve dec 21." In April old reliable "Topsy" was bred and expected to calve the following February. In one succinct entry, Joe wrote that "saria was screwed to day."[6]

Joe raised other calves as well. Since his cows gave much more milk then their own calves could drink, he bought additional calves from neighbors to raise. Melvin Mills "Brought Me [a] Bull calf today," Joe noted in July 1938, and in October he bought a calf from Otis Wheeler, paying "1.50 for it." Throughout the 1940s Joe continued buying calves from those around him. He got another calf from Melvin Mills in December, 1942 and the following July he "went over to Harry Harringtons" and bought a calf "for 2.50." In September Edwin Roberts brought three calves up to Joe and he "payed out 9.00 for them." Additional calves were routinely bought from the Howard brothers, who always had a slew of bull calves being born at the Udall barn, just down the road from Joe.[7]

Joe bought these calves to raise and sell. While he sold most of them when they had reached breeding or butchering age, he sometimes resold young calves when it was profitable. Almost certainly, the calves he sold were heifers, since dairy farmers wanted females to eventually milk much more than young bulls. In June 1938, Herbert Harrington came up to Joe's to buy a calf and the next year Joe "sold 2 ca[l]ves to Maxam for 20 dollars." Considering that bull calves went for $1.50 at the time, the two heifers he sold to Maxam must have been nice ones to bring ten dollars apiece. In 1943, Joe sold a bunch of calves. In March, one went "to [Arthur] longley for 20.00." In April another was sold to Melvin Mills ("he owes me 20.00"), and a week later he sold two more to Longley. In July he sold the last calf for that year, before buying three new ones to start over with.[8]

Most of the time, Joe sold older cattle. Sometimes he sold them butchered, as in December 1938 when he butchered one and sold parts of it to Miss Wood and Ted Paronto. The next fall, "harry Harrington came up to see [a] Beef [,] But i did not sell him any," evi-

Joe Ranger as photographed by Dan Brockway. Courtesy of David Brockway.

dently because they couldn't agree on a price. In early October 1942, Joe "sold 2 hed of young stock to fog [Fogg] for 150.00" and later in the month he "sold [a] heffer for 50.00 and 8 calves." In November he sold one of his cows "for 125.00 to Melvin Mills" and then a couple weeks later he replaced it, buying a "heffer for 50.00" from Melvin along with a calf.[9]

In the late 1940s, Joe was still buying and selling cattle, though he was winding down. In June 1949, he "sold 3 hed of cattle for 290.00" and later in the month another animal for $115.00. When he sold his bull during the summer of 1950 for $125.00, it appears that thereafter Joe kept only one cow for his own milk and to feed the pigs he kept.[10]

During the years that Joe kept cattle until 1949, he continued to exchange work with his neighbors. With his last entry in his 1921 diary, we lose track of Joe's work patterns through his own written record. Nevertheless, even though there is a seventeen-year gap in Joe Ranger's diaries for the period 1921-1937, he certainly kept working for his neighbors. During this time Joe aged from being 46 years old to 62. It would be natural to expect significant changes to have occurred during these years, influencing Joe's life and perhaps changing his earlier routine of working out so much. Nineteen hundred thirty seven, however, found Joe doing the same sort of work he had been doing seventeen years earlier. His daily diary entries and seasonal routines of farm and neighborhood varied little since the early 1920s. The only change seemed to be the cast of characters.

In Joe's earlier diaries, Dan and John Brockway, Sid Wheeler, Wallace Jennings, Walter Harrington, the Barrows, Arthur Ellis, Charles Wood, the Howards, and Albert Parker were the main people Joe interacted with. By the late 1930s they had been replaced by Otis Wheeler, Harry Harrington, Alice Wood, Ted Paronto, Lyle Adams, Melvin Mills, and Frank King. Only Albert Parker and the

Howards bridged the two periods. The change in neighbors was mainly generational. It is evident from the continuity of the surnames that Joe had sustained interaction with certain families. Otis Wheeler was Sid Wheeler's son, Harry Harrington was Walter Harrington's son, and Alice Wood was Charles Wood's daughter. Joe knew these people as children, and now he worked for them as adults.[11]

Joe also connected with the new owners of old farms he had worked on for previous owners. For instance, Melvin Mills lived on the farm earlier owned by Arthur Ellis. After Mills left and was replaced by Ward Starbuck, Joe worked for him too. Although from northern Vermont and new to the neighborhood, Ted Paronto worked for the Howard brothers a familiar enough family. Frank King had always lived on his place and Joe's work for him in the 1930s probably had more to do with Frank not needing the help before, but later relying on Joe and Joe's willingness to walk a little further for work.[12]

Joe chopped and split wood, drew manure, harrowed, cultivated corn, and hayed for Frank King in 1937, along with getting up firewood for Melvin Mills and the Starbucks.[13] The next year he did the same work: cut wood for Starbuck, the Howards, Otis Wheeler, and Alice Wood and hayed for Wood and Wheeler. He also hayed and cut corn for both Melvin Mills and Otis Wheeler.[14] In 1939 he cut corn for Otis and the Howards and later that fall he chopped wood thirty-four days for Ernest Howard.[15] He cut corn for the Howards in 1942 along with picking apples for Ralph Howard and in November, cut firewood for the Howards' neighbor, Frank Fogg.[16] Nineteen hundred forty three found Joe cutting wood for Otis in February and March and then helping Albert Parker get in his second cutting of hay in September. Come October, he cut corn for both Parker and Otis Wheeler.[17] Joe's 1944 diary is only partially extant,

70

but it finds him getting out ash logs for Otis in January and Parker in February and then helping tap Parker's sugar bush.[18]

As time passed, Joe could not keep up with his neighbors in laying out money for new equipment and larger herds. As a result, he could only offer his labor to his neighbors in return for work they did for him with their hired men, horse-drawn equipment, and special tools, as well as their own labor. Such an arrangement meant that Joe ended up working longer for his neighbors than they did for him.

By 1937, Joe was fully dependent on his neighbors for getting much of his large scale annual chores done. Because he no longer had a team of horses, he relied on everyone else around him. Once in a while Joe borrowed someone's team, but most of the time his neighbors drove the horses themselves when he needed them. Albert Parker, Otis Wheeler, and the Howards all hauled grain for Joe whenever he needed a load. Otis also drew wood for Joe and cultivated his potatoes with a horse-drawn cultivator.[19]

Over the years, various neighbors brought their horses and equipment down to help Joe during haying, as they were needed to pull the mowing machine, rake, and hay wagon. He used Harry Harrington and Melvin Mills' horses during the 1937 haying season.[20] Another year Otis brought his team and two hired boys to get in Joe's hay.[21] Albert Parker and his hired man helped Joe hay a few years later with Albert's team.[22]

While Joe's neighbors were willing to use their horses and machines working for Joe, they rarely provided only labor. When they did it was to immediately pay back like labor Joe had provided for them. One January Joe went over to help Frank King and a few days later Frank came to help Joe. When fence-fixing time came in the spring, four hands were better than only two: "helped Melvin... fix fence and he helped Me fix fence."[23]

Joe depended on his neighbors for help, but they really didn't have to help him that much. It didn't take very long to hay for Joe, for example, because only enough hay to sustain Joe's very small herd of cattle had to be put away for winter, while the other farmers needed to put up vast amounts for their larger herds. Joe had all the same kinds of chores as the others on his farm, but he required a lot less to be done. Thus, he was at a certain advantage in some respects when it came to trading work. While he provided lots of labor for others, in return he would get his manure spread on his fields, his hay cut and put away in the barn, his grain hauled, and his wood skidded out to his dooryard. It wasn't a bad deal since time was the one thing Joe had.[24]

Because Joe needed so little of his neighbor's time, he usually worked much more than they could pay him back in labor. So, instead of trading work, they paid him in cash like the times they specifically hired him for certain chores. Joe noted in his diary when his time was for cash or to be applied toward someone's account. One July, Ralph Howard came up to "hire" Joe "to Peal Basswood for him By the our," but this arrangement was rare in his work relationships with most of his neighbors.[25] Sometimes they owed him little as when Joe settled accounts with Harry Harrington in March 1937. They got together and figured out that Harry owed Joe $27.43 "for chopping" wood and that Joe owed Harry $26.85. Harry thus paid Joe fifty-eight cents to equal things up.[26]

Some accounts were relatively small; others involved a lot of time and money. When Joe got some bags of bran from Alice Wood in June 1939 for $3.20, he simply deducted that amount from what she owed him for work. He wasn't sure at the time what she owed him, so a couple days later he sat down and added up all the hours he had worked for her. He wrote down that the "Total [of] my acct again[st] Miss Wood to date is 153.80." After working for her another two months more the total increased to $227.15.[27]

Similar to his active years of dairying, sometimes Joe felt slighted when he traded work on an unequal footing with neighbors without being duly compensated for the extra work he ended up giving them. Tom Paronto recalled Joe and Otis Wheeler having a hard time keeping even and out of trouble with each other concerning work and money, particularly when it came to haying.[28] Joe's 1938 diary confirms Paronto's memory that Joe and Otis used to help each other haying. At the time, Otis was still working as farm manager for Alice Wood and in June and July, Joe noted helping hay down to Miss Wood's with Otis a total of twelve days. In the beginning of August he helped Otis get in oats for Miss Wood three different days, ending on the 14th. The next day Otis commenced helping Joe get in his own hay. They quickly worked up five loads with help from Melvin Mills. On the 16th, they also had two boys helping and got in six loads. Over the next several days Otis helped get in hay until the 21st, when Joe noted that they had finished, putting in "25 loads in all" that season with Otis contributing five days toward the effort. As soon as they finished haying Joe's farm they went up the next day to the farm where Otis had grown up and began haying there for Otis. Joe worked seven days on the Wheeler place helping Otis, some days putting in "8 ours" before they finished the job on August 31st. Joe had helped Otis twenty-two days haying while Otis had helped Joe only five days.[29]

What can not be gleaned from Joe's diaries is how he felt about this imbalance between himself and Otis Wheeler. He simply didn't write about it. But if he didn't complain about the situation, he eventually did do something about it. Tom Paronto recalls a story about Joe that makes the ultimate outcome of the haying dispute clear. Joe told Tom that "one year" he didn't go near Otis' or Miss Wood's when it came haying time. Expecting that he would want help with his hay, they naturally thought that he would come around to help them first. But he didn't. Evidently by the time they finished their own haying, they learned that Joe's haying was also all done. Surprised at hearing this and wondering how he could have got it done without Otis' annual help, they asked Joe, "who did your haying?" "Joe Armstrong," Joe replied. Bewildered, they asked who that was. "Me," Joe answered wittily, indicating that he and his strong arms had done all the haying alone.[30] Whether or not they believed Joe, the point was made that he was all done haying with them if he wasn't duly compensated for the extra time he spent helping them.

After selling most of his cattle in 1949, Joe turned his attention

Joe Ranger with berries from his plants. Photo: William Burch.

74

and time to raising fruit and flowers. He had always kept a garden, but it wasn't until the 1950s that he could expand his gardening to include an extensive berry patch. People fondly remember Joe's berries. Tom Paronto remembers both red and yellow raspberries. Damon Jillson claimed Joe had all sorts of berries, which he offered to people who stopped by his place.[31]

Joe's diary enables us to see just how much time and effort he expended on his berries. In 1957 he commenced working on his berry patch in May and continued dealing with them until August 22, when he "finished rasberrys."[32] The next year Joe spent April 14-16 fertilizing his berries and then between May and October he mentioned working on them on seventy-six different days. Word of Joe's success with berries spread. People wouldn't just stop in to buy berries, they also placed orders in advance. On May 31, 1958, Joe took an order for sixty-four boxes of raspberries.[33] A few people even hired him to work in their own berries, hoping his touch would work magic on their modest patches.[34]

Joe expanded his berry patch by allowing his own canes to spread, but he also ordered plants from catalog companies. In February 1959 he ordered $8.50 worth and then waited for their arrival in spring. The snow left early in March and Joe commenced fertilizing on the 24th. His new plants came and he mentioned finishing "setting out" the new ones on May 19th.[35] That season he mentioned berries eighty-three times in his diary, including working on them, picking them, cutting the grass between the rows, even paying "out 4.00 for help Picking Berries," and then in September getting Bob Moore to come and harrow-in a section of old canes in preparation for setting out new ones the following spring.[36] When Joe's diary ended for good in May 1960 he had already ordered fruit trees and more berry bushes that spring and had begun the cycle of tending the plants when he ceased writing. Although Joe didn't keep his diary after that point, his

75

check register for 1963 and 1964 indicates that he continued ordering more berry plants.[37]

Even though Joe continued to support himself by raising and selling berries, it was questionable during his last years if he could remain on his own. Neighbors noted Joe's struggles as he aged, and they helped out. Joe successfully applied for Old Age Assistance from the State's Department of Social Welfare, which provided money for those who were elderly and had no stable source of income. The program was not gratis, however. In return for the assistance, the state put a lien on the beneficiary's property, in essence taking whatever the person possessed at death. This system provided a safety net for a portion of the state's poorest citizens, and it no doubt helped Joe Ranger tremendously.[38]

The first mention in Joe's diary of the possibility of getting old age assistance was on February 19, 1949, and it was not through his own instigation. That day John Doton "came over to see about getting old age pension for me," Joe wrote with apparent surprise. Doton was one of Pomfret's three selectmen, and took the lead in seeing what could be done for Joe. Joe didn't hear back from Doton, but in late April the town clerk "came up to see about my old age pension." The clerk evidently was charged with making out the actual paperwork and getting Joe to sign it to start the application process.[39] Joe never pondered in his diary whether the application would be accepted or not. The days went by and Joe continued trying to keep his truant cattle in their pasture, attending auctions, visiting neighbors, and working for Alice Wood in her flower garden.[40]

When the first assistance check actually came in mid-October, Joe only noted that he "rec[eived] 30.00 in pension."[41] His muted celebration notwithstanding, the monthly old age assistance Joe received from the State of Vermont helped him to remain independent throughout his remaining years. It is hard to discern any measurable difference in Joe's lifestyle before and after he began getting the state money, but some things became apparent. For one thing, he began paying his property taxes. He had become delinquent in his town taxes, not having paid any since 1937. Joe began paying his taxes again in 1954 and this certainly was made possible by the extra income from the state. Once he started paying his property taxes again, he never missed a year for the rest of his life.[42]

The assistance money also replaced Joe's farm income. During the summer of 1949 he sold most of his cattle when it became apparent he would be receiving the state money. In June he "sold 3 hed" of cattle for 290.00 on the 5th and then on the 23rd sold another "cow."[43]

Although Joe Ranger changed some of his daily and seasonal routines after he began getting old age assistance, other things he kept right on doing. Even though he got rid of most of his cattle, he kept a cow for his own use, an old horse, and continued to raise pigs.

6

Character

In 1941, Joe Ranger appeared in a United States Department of Agriculture film entitled *Harvests For Tomorrow* as an example of a failed farmer. Joe had a very minor part, no more than a few seconds. These few seconds, however were very important: Joe represented decline and degeneracy.

Harvests For Tomorrow was produced to enlighten northern New Englanders to the problems of soil depletion and show the benefits of liming and fertilizing the region's acidic farmland. The film's narrator, Frank Craven, begins by informing the audience of its didactic nature: "There are no actors in this picture. These are plain people of farm and village. There is no plot. But there is a story." The story, he says, is "of the growth and decline and rebirth of New England's rocky" soil. In other words: the soil was good, man came along and depleted it, and now he must build it back up with lime and fertilizer.

The scene leading up to Joe's appearance begins with a shot of a "rich-looking valley, but as the camera begins to pan from left to right we slowly see land getting poorer and poorer until [the] camera stops and we see land that is completely worn out and covered by hardhack." Another shot shows a pasture growing up to hardhack and juniper with cows "eating very slightly." The narrator declares that, "The land's too poor for almost anything else, so the brush and the scrub take over. Brush and scrub - hard fare for cattle." Just before the scene switches to Joe, we see men throwing armfuls of corn over a fence to cattle in a worn out field so they will have something to eat. As the scene dissolves the narrator reflects on the situation: "Bad, anyway you look at it. That's the way it goes - the land runs down, the houses and barns run down and - well, the people run down." Then there he is: "Old Joe cutting brush in [a] worn out field." A couple more shots of Joe cutting brush "but from [a] different angle," and then he's gone. The next scene shows a set of dilapidated farm buildings and then continues to an auction scene and some more worn-out fields. "All of this is what happens when the land runs down," says the narrator. "Not very pretty. And the worst of it is it doesn't have to happen." The film goes on to show how worn out land can be improved by the addition of lime and fertilizer, and all ends happily for the local farmers, with the exception of Joe Ranger, apparently.[1]

To many living in the area, the film's content didn't matter. What mattered was that local people were featured in it. When it was shown in regional theaters, locals flocked to see the outcome of the previous year's filming of their friends and neighbors. From Hartford, Merton Nott and the Lymans appeared from the Jericho district and Ralph Stetson from West Hartford. Further up the valley, folks and scenes from South Royalton were also shown. People enjoyed watching those they knew appearing in the film as they plowed, hayed, cut corn, picked apples, spread lime and fertilizer, and sat down to dinner right there on the big screen.[2]

Of all the people who were in *Harvests For Tomorrow*, Joe Ranger was certainly not the most prominent. However, Joe appeared in the film not just because he was a failed farmer; there were plenty of them to film. What set Joe apart, and why he was specifically sought out for his role, was that he already had a local reputation. Joe was a "character."

Joe Ranger's identification as a local character took time and was enhanced by his particular attributes as the years passed. These peculiarities were of no threat to anybody and that is why they were tolerated and recounted by his neighbors. However, Joe's ways were different enough that people considered him in a category of his own.

One aspect that set Joe apart from most of his neighbors was that he lived alone and never married. That in itself was not especially notable. Many people in the area remained single all their lives. Neighbors Alice Wood, Otis Wheeler, Ralph Howard, Albert Parker, and Sophia King also never married. The difference, however, was that even though they did not marry, they didn't live alone. Alice Wood had Otis Wheeler as the hired man living in her household. After Wood's death, Wheeler's friends and family, as well as his own hired help, lived with him. Ralph Howard lived with brother Ernest's family on the old homestead. Albert Parker lived with his folks until their death. And even though many speculated that he would hook up with old Sophia King, he never did, but instead remained single and included farm workers in his household. Sophia King died alone on the farm she was born on, but not until after she outlived everybody else in the family.[3]

Joe, on the other, hand rejected family, or anybody else trying to live with him. Although we have seen how Joe's mother lived with him until moving to the town poor farm, some thought her departure was unnecessary. Burton Wheeler claimed that the reason Joe's mother didn't continue to live with him was not because of his inability to care for her, but because he wouldn't have her. According to Wheeler, Joe kicked his mother out of his house. While impossible to verify now, some who knew him thought it not past Joe to have done such a thing.[4]

Those who were too young to remember the details of Joe's mother's departure from his house, used his treatment of his sister Mary as their template for understanding Joe's preference for living alone. Mary married twice and both marriages failed and she lived alone in a number of different places over the years in various circumstances. One woman remembered Mary living in Lebanon, New Hampshire, chasing the youngsters who teased her about kissing a man they thought she liked. While battling delinquents and struggling to get by, Mary probably wanted to live out her later years with her only brother. He was family. He had his own place, she could keep the house clean, and he could do the outside work, making it pleasant for both of them. However long Mary Ranger imagined such fantasies, they never came close to reality. Joe kept her out.[5]

So, instead of moving in with Joe, Mary would visit him and stay for several days at a time. Sometimes she would get a ride to the neighborhood, but other times she would walk from wherever she was living at the time. In the end, she always left, either on her own, or with the help of Joe's boot.

It is easy to envision Joe being miserable to his sister while she was visiting him. Many who lived in the neighborhood remember Joe's actions toward, and antipathy for her. Joe himself admitted as much. He told Clifford Guthrie that he couldn't stand living with his sister, claiming that she "lived different than I do." In other words, she would try to clean his place up. Dennis Clay remembers Joe telling Dennis and his father that he and his sister "didn't see eye to eye." They could have guessed that because whenever Joe mentioned his sister, he "didn't speak highly of her."[6]

Tom Paronto saw firsthand how Joe treated his sister while she was staying with him because one summer day Tom was driving by and stopped to see Joe. Tom had his dog with him and while Joe and Tom were visiting it chased after one of the cats. Mary saw this and began berating the dog. Tom recalled that Joe turned to her and bellowed out, "you son-of-a-bitch, you shut your mouth." After that, Tom said, "she weren't there only a few more days" before going home.[7] Joe Ranger liked visitors, not housemates.

Because Joe was poor and he could not afford to modernize, he never owned, or even drove, an automobile. While he did have a horse for years, Joe mainly traveled by foot. After his active farming years, he used to walk everywhere he went. While occasionally making his way beyond the bounds of the neighborhood, Joe mainly walked the Qucchee-North Pomfret-West Hartford triangle. Walking had been a time-honored mode of travel in the region, but the automobile changed all that. In addition to commuting to work, many people who used to walk to the village or to visit a friend, now drove a car. Even though Joe walked, he always accepted a ride when asked, though people remember him walking than riding. Joe stuck to his pedestrian ways even in his old age.

Everyone living along Joe's route remembers him walking by. They recall that he almost always carried a stick over his shoulder with a bag on the end, hobo style. Indeed, this habit reminded older folks of the period before the 1940s when real hobos made their way through the neighborhood begging, or offering to trade work for a meal. But for Joe, the stick and bag was a practical way to carry items he bought at the village store. Nonetheless, Joe looked to many like an old hobo.[8]

Along with lacking an automobile, Joe also never had electricity. He never appeared to want it. Even if he had, it would have been impractical to run electric lines all they way from the old Brockway place to his house. He wasn't interested in generating his own electricity like many local farmers before electrification became widespread. Instead, Joe cooked on a woodstove. He milked his cows by hand instead of by machine. And he moved in the night by the glow of kerosene lamps instead of light bulbs.

The other modern convenience everybody else but Joe acquired was running water. The house did not have a cistern and was never plumbed. Joe got his water from the nearby brook. There was a place where he bailed out water down the road from his house where the stream ran under the road. Whenever he needed water he would walk down to the head of the culvert, dip his pail in, haul up the bucket full, and carry it back to the house if for himself, or to the barn for his livestock. Joe may have hauled a lot of water up from the brook, but he never wasted any of it on a bath.[9]

Perhaps the most distinctive thing about Joe Ranger to most of those who knew him was the fact that he was the dirtiest cuss around. He and his house were utterly filthy. One of the earliest firsthand accounts epitomizing Joe's reputation in the area as being dirty comes from Scott Harrington. One day when Scott was a kid, he and his parents were out for a ride in their buggy. They had gone up to Bunker Hill and then down the road toward Joe's place. When they got there Joe came out of his house "with a piece of strawberry short-cake he'd made" to give to Scott's mother. "Well mister," remembered Scott, "it was in a dish that had never been washed I don't think and he handed it to mother. I remember that just as plain...[and] she accepted it." After visiting with Joe a bit, the Harringtons went along their way. When "we got down the road a ways," Scott said, his mother "threw it off into the ditch." That was the first time Scott Harrington *ever* saw Joe Ranger.[10] Joe's filth impressed young and old alike.

The Harringtons weren't the only ones to forgo eating food prepared by Joe. Pete Clifford was once over to Joe's with another fellow during Prohibition when Joe was selling hard cider. Joe was in the middle of eating dinner, but got up to get the pair some cider. The other fellow had a drink, but Pete decided "after seeing [Joe's] plate, I wasn't thirsty."[11]

Burton Wheeler also wouldn't drink, or eat, anything at Joe's. One summer when Burt was young, helping Joe hay, it came lunch time. Before anything was said, Burt quit what he was doing and ran all the way home to eat his lunch. Later he ran all the way back. Upon returning, Joe asked him where he went. After Burton told him, Joe said that was silly, he would have gotten something for Burt to eat. Burt didn't say what he did about dinner the other days he helped hay.[12] Probably he brought his lunch and most certainly he did not eat Joe's food.

When Henry Small was a teenager in the early 1960s and working for Otis Wheeler, Joe offered him some food while Henry was visiting with him. Joe was eating near-raw salt pork and washing it down with Four Roses. Joe offered Henry some and when Henry refused, Joe snickered, teasing Henry.[13] Joe Ranger knew right well that he wouldn't get anybody to eat anything he fixed.

Others also remembered Joe's filthy dining accommodations. Walt Howard, Burt Wheeler, and Erwin Clifford among others all commented on them. It was said that Joe never washed his dish, he just took a piece of bread and wiped it in a circular motion and ate the bread, leaving the plate on the table with its rim of moldy grime for the next meal.[14]

It was even hard for some people to eat in Joe's presence. Scott Harrington and Tom Paronto would stop by and eat their sandwiches with Joe once in a while when they were over that way working on the road, but not many others did. Tom had grown up knowing Joe and later he worked for the Pomfret Highway Department with Harrington. Tom figured Joe would like the company, so he would make it a point to stop by if he was in the neighborhood. One time

Tom had fellow employee, Raymond Longley, with him. Tom parked the truck near Joe's and told Raymond to grab his lunchbox and come in. Joe welcomed them in, but Raymond only got as far as the doorway. Tom said that when Raymond saw the mess, he turned right around and ate his lunch in the truck, leaving Tom to eat and visit with Joe. From then on, whenever Raymond was with Tom over that way and Tom would stop to see Joe, Raymond begged him not to stay too long.[15]

The mess at Joe's that made Raymond Longley sick got people's attention. When Joe got older, Tom Paronto said, he would step just outside the door, pull down his pants, and "just shit off the [door]step." Joe once had a horse that died out in the field nearby and Joe left him right there. Over the summer it got pretty rank smelling. When the Howards were over near Joe's and smelled the stench, they told him he should bury the horse. Joe just shrugged and said that it would go away after a while.[16]

The inside of Joe's house elicited considerable comment. Describing the first time he went inside Joe Ranger's house, Erwin Clifford said that the kitchen table "was as far as you could go." There were cans, cartons, garbage, "you name it," piled all around, filling the rest of the room, and presumably, the rest of the house. Walt Howard also only ever got as far as Joe's kitchen because of boxes and stuff thrown everywhere else. Walt wondered at the time how Joe ever got into his other rooms. The answer was, he didn't. Joe lived in his kitchen. The Parontos remember only a path from the doorway to the little corner where Joe had a table, bed, and stove. In the winter, Joe also had firewood inside, piled all around up to the ceiling. Tom remembers broken windows loosely covered with old burlap bags through which rodents and cats freely traveled. In one corner, inside the wall partition, lived a swarm of bees. Several people remember them and that sometimes when the bees were disturbed Joe would have to get out of the house and go to his little shed by the road until they calmed down. While no one has any recollection of the upstairs of Joe's house, at least one person got a glimpse of his cellar. Otis Wheeler said it was "full of trash."[17]

Those who stopped at Joe Ranger's house saw first-hand the filth he lived in; many more witnessed his lack of personal hygiene. By walking everywhere he went, Joe came into contact with most of the region's residents at some time or other. Folks all along the road to West Hartford saw Joe walk by. North Pomfret's residents knew him by sight. And practically everyone in Quechee encountered Joe. Along with pedestrian travel, business dealings in the village general stores exposed townspeople to Joe. Carolyn Toby told about the first time she saw Joe Ranger. She was a teenager getting off the school bus at Finley's store in West Hartford and saw a dirty-faced old man with tobacco-stained whiskers in filthy clothes trudging his way to the store. Even though she had never seen Joe Ranger before, she knew it was him. She had heard about Joe through family and neighbors and never having encountered anybody like this guy before, knew it must be him.[18]

Carolyn Toby was astonished by Joe Ranger, because of how dirty he actually was. While daily baths in the 1930s and 1940s were rare for many, nobody was as dirty as Joe. One fall in the early 1930s when Erwin Clifford was a kid, his father Gerald needed help with the plowing and hired Joe Ranger to come and do it. The younger Clifford remembered sitting on the bank and watching Joe plow the field, but he also vividly remembered the ruckus Joe caused at dinner time. Clifford's mother provided Joe with dinner and made quite a fuss over Joe's dirty hands when he came in to eat. Clifford said that Joe went outside to the water pump and tried "to wash them but they were so caked and dirty [that] the hide would have come off if the dirt came."[19]

Along with dirty hands, people remember many other aspects of Joe's filth. His face was so dirty it provided a dark background for his bright eyes. When he spoke, he would spit tobacco juice. What didn't spray the poor listener, dribbled from the corners of his mouth onto his scraggly beard. Many said that Joe never changed his clothes, he would just put on another pair right over the old ones, which apparently rotted away with time. Evidently, the old clothes got pretty dirty before it was time to put on new ones. Walt Howard said Joe's pants were so dirty with dirt and pine pitch that they "had a shine to them." Not many people ever said that Joe shined.[20]

People said Joe was so dirty because he almost never bathed. Erwin Clifford remembers Joe saying that when he took a bath he would lay down in the brook with his clothes on. Joe "had a saying," one neighbor claimed, "you should have a bath once a year." "So," she concluded, "he fell in the brook once a year." Dennis Clay's memory contradicts this, however. He remembers Joe saying that he would jump in the pond *twice* a year. However many times Joe got wet, he never got clean.[21]

As dirty as Joe was, he was still welcomed inside people's homes. Irene Brockway claimed that when Joe left her place from a visit, she would have to clean the doorknobs. Even so, she always let him come visit. When asked if she used to let Joe in her own house, Alvina Harrington retorted, "Absolutely, he was a human being just like the rest of us." She admitted that "he didn't keep very clean but that's alright." And if "we had food I'd give it to him" even at the kitchen table. Even when Joe was welcome and accepted, his hosts still marveled at how dirty he was.[22]

Those who knew Joe Ranger only by sight may have assumed that he was stupid because he was dirty. However, if these same people ever had a conversation with Joe, they may have changed their minds. "He was a smart man," remembered Scott Harrington while reminiscing about Joe in July, 2001. "Everybody said the same thing." But while people who knew Joe said he was smart, they had a hard time explaining the nature of his intelligence. He had only a few years of schooling. His experiences were provincial. He lived in poverty. Despite these traits, Joe impressed those who got to know him. While appearing ignorant, one "could tell by visiting with him" that he knew what he was talking about.[23]

Joe knew what he was talking about in part because he read so much. His knowledge of the Bible impressed people. While Joe was never remembered as having set foot in a church, he "read the Bible and could repeat many passages." No doubt, Joe Ranger probably was more familiar with the tenets of Christianity than many of his neighbors. Alvina Harrington certainly thought he could hold his own in a religious debate. She concluded that Joe "had to be a brilliant man to read the bible and quote [it] like he did."[24]

Joe read more than the Bible. He was forever telling stories from the books he read, impressing his listeners. One of Joe's favorite authors was Zane Grey. After spending many winter days inside by his stove reading, in the summer Joe reveled in sharing what he read with visitors. Those who stopped to see Joe were there only a while before Joe got going on Zane Grey. Unfortunately, folks don't remember the specifics of what Joe said about the novels he read. It would be interesting to know, for example, if Joe discussed more than the contents of the story itself. Did he consider the author's style or use of language as he read and later spoke of what he read? Nobody remembers. What they do remember was the plain fact that Joe read all the time and discussed what he read. For many, that in itself was enough to qualify him as smart.[25]

Joe was also a master at the game of witty responses. Most of his wit was focused on the everyday, mundane events of the neighborhood. One cold winter morning when it was well below zero and Joe walked to Finley's store in West Hartford, Mr. Finley inquired how cold it was at Joe's place. Joe responded that he couldn't really tell because he had a broom leaned against the wall under the thermometer and the mercury was halfway down the broomstick.[26]

For a number of years Joe had an old dog and then people noticed that the dog wasn't around anymore. One day Jim Clay asked Joe what had happened to the dog. Well, Joe said, he was told that the dog needed to have shots to protect it from rabies. Joe didn't think much of that. The dog was fine. He also was informed that if he didn't get his dog vaccinated and it bit someone, it would have to be put down and tested for rabies. Joe thought it cruel to have the dog vaccinated. So he decided to take care of the matter himself, as he told Clay. "I had to kill the dog to save his life."[27]

Another comeback that Jim Clay's son, Dennis, never forgot was the first spring when Joe came back home from living at the old Burch house in North Pomfret. Joe came walking down by the Clays' place and stopped to visit with Jim and Dennis. Not having seen Joe since the fall and knowing that he had been over at North Pomfret that winter, Jim Clay asked Joe how he liked the Burch house. "Dirtiest damn place I've ever lived in, Jim," was Joe's response.[28] Father and son chuckled over that one and spread it around town.

Although Joe was mainly noted for his wit in humorous encounters with his neighbors, there also was another side to his wit. Scott Harrington claimed that "Joe was nobody's fool." It was rare when somebody got the better of Joe. Through everyday interaction with Joe, his neighbors learned firsthand that he was, indeed, no fool. In fact, some learned the hard way that Joe Ranger was more than a match for them.[29]

Earle Harrington had trusted Joe for a bill at his store in North Pomfret one time. As the weeks went by, Harrington wondered when he would get paid. Although Earle hadn't said anything about the bill, Joe knew Earle was itching for his money. Perhaps miffed at the thought that Earle questioned whether he would ever get his money, Joe tricked Earle, confronting the issue head on to his own advantage. "Earle, are you worried about that bill I owe you?" Joe asked Earle one day he happened to be at the store. Probably being a bit embarrassed, Earle replied that no, he wasn't worried. Good, replied Joe, "Keep right on not worrying," and out the door he went. "Goddam him," Earle said, "I'll get even with him for that one."[30] No one heard that he ever did.

While Joe tricked Earle Harrington, he humiliated Albert Sherburne. Sherburne was a native of Pomfret and connected to the town's elite. A successful farmer, some thought him rather grasping in his dealings with others. Sherburne was active in town politics and didn't mind pursuing town business, that would also benefit his own position. Albert knew Joe Ranger was behind in his taxes and one time he tried to collect on the debt. Joe was raising calves, getting bull calves from the Howard brothers and raising them up for beef. One day, the Howards gave Joe a couple of heifer calves that were the daughters of heifers, thus not to be kept, in their estimation. It wasn't long before word got to Albert Sherburne that Joe had two jersey heifer calves. Thinking that he could take Joe's calves in the name of the town and then redeem them for himself for a little of nothing, Sherburne legally attached the calves. The day came for the calves to be taken and Albert showed up at Joe's big as life with the sheriff. The sheriff went into the barn to bring the calves out. But when he got in there he yelled to Sherburne, "Albert, I thought you attached heifers." "I did," replied Sherburne. The sheriff, somewhat amused, yelled back that they weren't heifers, "not by a damn sight," adding, "You'd better pick up his tail and look." Sure enough, it was a bull calf, and the other one was too. Unknown to Sherburne and the others, Joe had earlier brought the heifer calves back down to the

Howard brothers' barn at the Udall place, left them and brought back home two bull calves. Sherburne was furious. "I'll get even with you Joe Ranger for that," he roared. Joe just laughed. "It'll be a long day in hell before you do, Mr. Sherburne. You ain't smart enough," Joe retorted. Angry and humiliated at being beaten, Albert Sherburne quit his position as selectman that day, saying he wasn't going to serve in order to have people make a fool out of him. Many in Pomfret recounted this story with especial glee.[31]

Other gleeful stories about Joe recounted by his neighbors centered around Joe feeling wronged and getting back at his transgressors. One year Albert Parker was planning on going to the state fair in Rutland and told Joe about the trip. Joe instantly said that he would like to go along. Albert told Joe to be at the farm at 7:00 the next morning if he was going. Although it is not clear what time Joe showed up the next morning, it was close to 7:00 a.m. When he got there, Albert had already gone. Albert certainly could have taken a minute or two to drive over to Joe's to see if he was going, but he hadn't. More than likely, Albert didn't care to have Joe come along. At any rate, Joe was so mad that he went out into Albert's melon patch and smashed every single one of his melons, and then walked back home.[32]

Joe also got back at the Howard brothers for times he figured he was wronged by them. One year the Howards' young cattle got out of the pasture near Joe's place and trampled around in his potato piece, destroying most of his growing plants. Joe didn't make a big deal about the incident to the Howards, expecting them to make it right with him. They didn't, however. Perhaps they didn't realize the extent of the damage their cattle had caused at Joe's. At any rate, nothing more was said about the incident. Joe fumed and made a plan. The Howards had their own potato piece at the Udall place. That fall when the potatoes had got good-sized and before the

Howards dug them, Joe helped himself to them. Every couple days he went into the piece and dug out the spuds by hand from the potato hills, leaving behind no evidence of intrusion. By the time the Howards got around to dig the potatoes, Joe had filled his own bin. On the day Ernest Howard was digging the potatoes, Joe stopped by. Surveying the piece, Joe slyly commented that it didn't look like the crop had done very well. "No," Ernest guessed it hadn't. "Well," Joe said, "What I had that [your] cattle didn't ruin did real well."33 If Ernest Howard previously didn't know what had happened to his potatoes, he did then. After that, the Howards raised their potatoes at their home farm.

Ralph Howard also got Joe mad once, when Joe asked if he could have a tooth off an old spring-tooth harrow rusting away out in back of the barn at the Udall place. Ralph could have easily let Joe have it, but said no. Nothing more was said, but years later when Joe recounted this story to Ralph's nephew, Walt, Joe said that the tooth came up missing.34

Joe also impressed folks with his ability to sing. People were astonished when they heard sweet songs come from this dirty little man. Ted Paronto first heard Joe sing one day back in the 1930s when Ted was working up in the woods near Joe's with Ernest Howard. The pair were working on drawing out pulp wood when all of a sudden a beautiful voice echoed in the valley. Ted asked Ernest who the hell that could be, singing like that? It was Joe Ranger, Ernest replied, and he recalled that when they were kids at school, at recess time Joe and his sister Mary would hold hands and walk around the schoolhouse singing songs.

Erwin Clifford was also surprised by Joe's singing. During one deer hunting season in November, Clifford had walked from Bunker Hill to the old Wheeler place to sit and wait for a deer early one morning. He had just got himself situated in a good spot around day-

93

light when Joe Ranger came out of his house and yodeled and sang for a few minutes before starting his chores. Clifford sat there amazed. Years later he couldn't remember how the hunting was that day, but the singing was unforgettable.35

Not many people remember the songs Joe sang, but Burt Wheeler recalled Joe singing "Indian Love Call" and "Redwing" among others. It is easy to imagine Joe taking requests from those eager to hear him sing. He didn't only sing at home. According to Pete Clifford, Joe would "sing a song or two" anywhere, especially "if there were any women around. Guess he wanted to attract their attention." Ironically, with Joe's appearance and demeanor, Clifford concluded, he already had their attention without having to sing.36

Indeed, Joe loved to pay attention to women. The problem was that they didn't necessarily want his attention. Some husbands thought it funny to go out for a ride with family and friends and end up driving to Joe's for a visit so he could see their wives. Some women wouldn't get out of the automobiles when their husbands pulled into Joe's yard. That didn't matter, however, Joe would come out of his house and go right up to the side of the car the women were sitting on and stick his head in the window to talk with them. He liked to hold their hands or pat their shoulders as he talked. One woman claimed that "Joe would paw [you] all over if [you] let him," adding that Joe never touched her.37

Many women recoiled from Joe, but some accepted his filth and literally, embraced him just the same. On one visit to Joe's, Lois Brockway stunned her sister-in-law when she allowed Joe to hug her and she hugged him back.38

A group of high school girls who had heard about old Joe and his reputation decided that they would drive up to visit him under the guise of conducting a paper drive to raise money for school. They got together and made their way to Joe's place. Once there, they got out of the car and Joe came out of his house. While the sequence of events is not exactly clear, it appears Joe realized the girls had come up to tease him, so then turned the tables on them. He wanted to give them all a kiss and approached the first girl to do so. She screamed and ran around the side of the car. Turning to another girl, Joe forced her to climb over the hood to get away from him. After they had all got back into the car and locked the doors, they spun away, never to return.[39]

Perhaps the most enigmatic aspect of Joe Ranger's life was the relationship he established with a pair of beaver, which inhabited the pond across the road from his house. Dating their arrival is impossible, but before the early 1950s when the beaver came to the swamp and built a dam and a lodge, they were considered a relative rarity in the area. The days had long since passed when multiple beaver ponds dotted the streams of the old forested landscape of the 18th century. Draining swampy areas, clearing the land of trees, and trapping by humans together resulted in a drastic diminishment of the beaver population throughout the early 19th century, so that by the time Joe was alive it was an event when someone saw a beaver in the area.[40] Joe was very protective of his new neighbors. When people came poking around looking to possibly trap the beaver, Joe promptly let them know no one was going to trap *his* beaver. One time when one of the Clay boys was exploring the pond and walking around on the dam, Joe showed up and gave him hell, telling him to stay off the dam and lodge.[41]

It didn't take long for Joe's interest in the beaver to be known. Folks commented on the care he showed toward his furry friends and soon stories began making the rounds of Joe and the beaver. Some said he talked to them. While no one ever claimed the beaver spoke to Joe, several people witnessed Joe speak to them. In fact, some said he could call the beaver and they would emerge from their lodge and swim toward the edge of the pond where Joe stood.[42]

While many told of Joe's ability to call the beaver, most said they never saw it happen themselves. The experience of one pushy woman was probably typical for those needing proof. She showed up at Joe's one day with her two small children demanding to see Joe's beaver. Joe took the children across the road toward the pond, but when the mother marched herself right behind them, Joe turned and snapped, "No, you stay here." Joe and the kids were gone for some time and then returned. Even though the woman didn't (and still doesn't) know if her children actually saw any beaver, they believed they had.[43]

A story from the time Joe was being filmed for *Harvests for Tomorrow* gives us a glimpse of Joe's wit, and, love of liquor. Evidently, the director of the film indicated that he wanted to film Joe cutting brush in his field. That was all right, but Joe requested that he have

Joe Ranger at his beaver pond. Photo: William Burch.

something to drink while he worked. He insisted on alcohol. Obliging, they gave Joe a drink and he set to work cutting. After a little while, however, he stopped. The director told Joe that he wanted him to continue cutting brush. Joe told him he wouldn't until he had another drink. And so the filming went on, alternating between shots of film and shots of liquor.[44]

Drinking was an activity Joe Ranger was noted for. This in itself was not necessarily distinct to Joe. Drinking to excess was an accepted activity for many in the region. Pete Clifford recounted that when he was a child he couldn't tell if his father and the men who came over to play cards were always drunk, or just naturally acted the way they did. Practically every man in Pomfret drank, with hard cider being the popular choice.[45]

What set Joe apart was that he made his own hard cider long after many others had given up. When he had his own team, he would haul apples to a local cider mill where they were crushed and pressed and the resulting cider barreled before being brought back home. Later on when he no longer had a team, Joe got others to haul the apples for him. The cider was put in his cellar where it "worked" and after it had fermented it was ready to drink.

Joe's cider was well known throughout the neighborhood. Many partook. "People would gather up there" at Joe's "for no good reason, I'm afraid," recalled Alvina Harrington. "That's a polite way to put it." Harrington's father and husband frequented Joe's place. Reminiscing about Joe's cider, Ted Paronto claimed, "There ain't an old guy in Pomfret that hadn't had some of Joe's cider." Ted could also have included those in West Hartford and Quechee.[46]

Joe loved nothing more than to get someone drunk at his place and send him home. Melvin Mills used to spend time at Joe's drinking and usually had a hard time getting back over the hill. It was reported that after one particular drinking session, Melvin left Joe's and fell three times—between Joe's house and the road. Mills had quite a hike to make, but he eventually did make it home.[47]

Joe was quite willing to share cider with those who came to visit and drink, but he did not have an unlimited supply. Walt Howard remembers Joe putting up three barrels. Although one might think that amount should keep someone in drink, Joe had to be careful about doling out his precious stash. He would give someone he wanted to get drunk all they wanted, but when it came to someone just stopping by without the intention of getting loaded, Joe could be stingy.[48]

One time when the Howards were drawing out pulp from their lot above Joe's, he gave some cider to the workers hauling the pulp down by his place. They liked it so much, they decided to stop by the next trip they made and get another drink. Joe obliged. Soon they decided that they should stop every time they passed Joe's, on their way to get a load of pulp as well as when they hauled one out. Finally, they had had enough. One young fellow, however, said he wanted some more of that cider. They made one more stop at Joe's and when they came inside, Joe said, "Yep, I'm going to let you have one more glass and then, goddam you, you get home." The young guy was sick the next day.[49]

Joe worried he would run out of cider. Tom Paronto stopped by Joe's once to visit and have a glass of cider and didn't get a drop. Joe told him that his supply was getting low and Tom couldn't have any. Joe claimed that if he wasn't careful with what cider was left he would have to drink water before the next batch was ready. Precious as it was, Joe Ranger's cider met the lips of many in the neighborhood, and beyond.[50]

Joe's notoriety as a character eventually transcended his own neighborhood. It was through Joe's hard cider during Prohibition, however, that people from outside the neighborhood first got to know

98

him. A friend of a neighbor of Joe's would show up at Joe's door looking for a taste of cider. Later this friend would tell another friend and a web of knowledge of Joe spread out of the neighborhood and into the surrounding area. Because more and more people ended up coming to Joe's for cider, he was careful about getting set up and arrested for making and selling alcohol.

One day a fellow who Joe rightly suspected of being a lawman came to his door asking to buy some cider. After visiting a bit with the fellow, Joe disappeared and came back with a jug. The man paid Joe and went out the door. After getting down the road a way, he uncorked the jug and took a swig. Immediately he spit out what he hadn't swallowed and threw the jug down in the road. It was vinegar. Although this fellow had actually come for cider for himself and not to set up Joe, Joe was taking no chances.[51]

Along with his cider, Joe's berries also drew people from out of the neighborhood to his place. As Joe enlarged his berry beds every year, he was able to sell or give away more berries than just to those living nearby. Stella Bond from West Lebanon, New Hampshire, got to know Joe through his berries. Bond didn't raise any berries herself, but loved them. She raved about Joe's berries, but after meeting him, Bond washed the berries she bought from Joe with dish detergent. Through word of mouth, more and more people heard about Joe Ranger and his berries.[52]

Some claim Joe wouldn't give away berries to the locals, but instead saved them for those he had never met who stopped by. Melvin Young felt the same way. Richard Brockway had been up to see Joe toward the end of one strawberry season and saw a mass of juicy red strawberries, unpicked. Later, when visiting with Young, Brockway encouraged Young to go up to Joe's and get some before they rotted. Young and his wife went right up with empty tubs. Instead of being given any strawberries, however, they were met with

Joe's statement that he "was going to let them get a little more ripe" before picking them. Undoubtedly, the great majority of the berries sat there until they rotted into the ground. Joe was very particular about those to whom he sold and gave away berries. Over the years this increasingly meant people he hadn't previously known.[53]

Regardless of the cider or berries, Joe's friends and neighbors were mainly responsible for introducing new people to him. They had grown up knowing Joe and his peculiarities and shared their stories of Joe with people who had never heard of him. Naturally, many of the folks who heard these stories wanted to see Joe for themselves. Because of neighbors, their relatives and friends, as well as newcomers, Joe became known outside the West Hartford-Quechee-North Pomfret triangle. By the 1950s, Joe Ranger had been found.

Walt Howard was one person who introduced Joe to others from outside the area. Walt grew up on the family place in West Hartford and worked through his youth for his father and uncle on the farm. Walt's brother, John, was slated to take over the farm so Walt sought work in Windsor, Vermont, where he ended up working at the Goodyear plant for over twenty-four years. He married a Hartford girl, and made a home in nearby Hartland. He kept in contact with Joe over the years, dropping by to visit when he was up that way.

Walt also told his Brooks in-laws about Joe Ranger. The older folks were interested in the stories of Joe's cider and asked Howard to buy some for them. Walt obliged and as time went by, his in-laws were treated to other stories about Joe. After hearing about him for some time, they decided they wanted to meet him and see where he kept his cider. Walt and his wife made an outing one day, taking her parents to see Joe Ranger. The folks had been primed to expect his place to be messy, but it horrified Mrs. Brooks so much that for a while she wanted no more of Joe's cider. But they got to hear some of his stories firsthand. They marveled at his living conditions and found him quite "entertaining." Once they got back home, they must have related what they saw to their Windsor neighbors.[54]

Damon Jillson is another person who brought his friends up to meet Joe. Jillson had grown up in South Pomfret and knew Joe from the days when Joe used to walk over the hills to the annual auctions held at the Maxham farm. Jillson talked to Joe, knew where he lived, and stopped by to see him occasionally.

Later, after spending time in the military and marrying, Jillson and his wife settled in Somerville, Massachusetts, where they raised a family. Over the years Jillson told his kids stories about Joe Ranger and they got to meet him. The Jillsons always came to Vermont for vacations and to see family in Pomfret. One important part of the vacation was a day set aside to go visit Joe. The Jillson children were not as taken with Joe as their father was. They were scared of him. Joe would talk to them and pat them, but they recoiled. It wasn't until they got older that they actually wanted to see Joe Ranger.

Damon Jillson also brought Somerville friends and co-workers up to see Joe. Whenever the Jillsons returned from a Vermont trip they talked about it, and they told stories about Joe Ranger. "Most people down there" in Somerville couldn't imagine someone living as primitive as Joe did, Jillson recalled. "I would tell them about [Joe] and they wouldn't believe it." They would say "Ah, nobody lives like that." "Well," I said, "they do too." At least Joe did. "Oh no, no, no" they would respond incredulously. Eager to prove to his friends the truth about Joe, Jillson took them to Vermont to meet him. When they arrived "they couldn't believe it," Jillson said "Joe was good to them," and he accommodated by showing the visitors his berries, his beaver pond, and the inside of his house. All the while, Joe was telling them about what he did during the day, details about his garden or animals, or telling some story. The visitors loved it.[55]

Before leaving, "they all wanted to take pictures with him." As a result, through the pictures and their own stories about Joe, these friends of the Jillsons spread the word about Joe Ranger to their own friends and relatives in Massachusetts.[56]

The Brockways were another family who introduced new people to Joe. When Dan Brockway's son Richard left the area after a stint in the Air Force in World War II, he followed his brother, Henry, to the Boston area. There he settled, later working as an insurance adjuster and parts salesman for thirty-five years. Not long after arriving in Boston, Richard got to know his co-workers pretty well. In particular, he got to know one of the secretaries in the office where he worked. Lois Carey was from Watertown and received Brockway's attention with interest. By 1953, they were going out steady.

Naturally, Richard told Lois about growing up in the West Hartford-Quechee area, highlighting events, places, and people, including Joe Ranger. He related how Joe had worked for his father on the family's farm before the Depression. He also told about Joe's appearance, lifestyle, and stories. By the time the couple made their first trip to Quechee to visit Richard's parents, Lois had heard much about Joe Ranger.

When Richard brought Lois up to see Joe for the first time, she had heard all about how Joe lived off by himself, walked everywhere, and didn't wash. She knew Joe's place wouldn't be much, she later recounted, but "then I saw it for myself – I couldn't believe that somebody could possibly live like that." She had wondered how much of what Richard had told her was true. Most of it was. Joe was filthy, there were chickens picking around the floor of his house, stuff piled up all around. What really surprised her, however, was Joe was "happy to see us." He was really friendly. Also knowledgeable. He told Lois all about his beaver and recited some poetry for her. By the time she and Richard left Joe's, she had concluded that Joe could almost be called "worldly." "I didn't expect that," she later recalled.

After that first trip, Richard brought Lois up to Quechee "a lot." Many of these trips included further visits with Joe Ranger. Richard and Lois later married and spent their working years in the Boston area, no doubt telling their friends about Vermont and Joe Ranger.[57]

While Richard Brockway left the Quechee area, his brother Dan stayed. Dan Brockway and his Packard brothers-in-law were also responsible for bringing friends from elsewhere to visit Joe. The Packards knew Joe through his walks in the village and because he worked in a neighbor's flower beds. Naturally, they got to know him pretty well.

Dan Brockway married Irene Packard in 1948. When Irene's brothers grew up and moved away from Quechee, they kept their memories of Joe Ranger. Living in Oxford, Massachusetts, Kingston Packard told friends who had never been to Vermont about Quechee and Joe, suggesting that they should come up to Quechee with him to visit and "see how people live in Vermont." Irene Brockway remembers the glee her brothers took in bringing visitors to Joe Ranger's. "That's the first place they'd take these people from the city – because people don't believe it – until they see it."[58] Thanks to the Packards, Brockways, Jillsons, Howards, and others, many who would never have come into contact with Joe Ranger got to meet him and judge for themselves what kind of a character he was.

7

Newcomers

Knowledge of Joe Ranger also spread when newcomers began buying old farms in the neighborhood for second homes. This phenomena was part of a larger pattern throughout the region and Vermont, which helped lift many depressed farm neighborhoods out of poverty and brought a new host of people into contact with local characters like Joe Ranger.

Vermont had tried attracting newcomers to the state since the late 1880s. At first, state leaders focused on attracting new farmers. When the farmers didn't come, officials turned to promoting the region's natural wonders and the state's mountains and lakes as a vacation destination. The effort was intensified with the creation of a State Publicity Bureau in 1911 and the production of brochures highlighting Vermont as a place to come to for activities like hiking, camping, fishing, swimming, boating, and skiing.[1]

In addition to attracting vacationers, the State also sought to attract those who might become part-time residents in the rural communities. Officials wanted to spread the prosperity beyond the popular destination enclaves and into the farm neighborhoods.

The first publications produced to draw attention to Vermont's farms and summer homes were simply lists of properties for sale organized by county and town. While they informed prospective buyers about country properties, they did little to articulate why one should purchase them.[2]

The most successful promotional booklet convincing people to buy Vermont property was *Summer Homes* by Vermont writer Dorothy Canfield Fisher. *Summer Homes* was very different from the pedantic listings in previous booklets published by the Publicity Bureau. There was not one house listed for sale in it. Instead it was "An Open Letter," a chat really, describing the opportunities and advantages of owning rural Vermont property and how to go about acquiring it.

Summer Homes addressed a different audience. It targeted "those who earn their living by a professionally trained use of their brains" and "those others not technically of that class but who enjoy the kind of life usually created by professional people." In other words, "the better sort." With the publication of *Summer Homes*, and in 1946, the inauguration of the magazine *Vermont Life*, the State of Vermont helped facilitate a migration of urban professionals from out of state in the years after the Great Depression.[3]

And come they did. One of the most sought-after regions was the area around Woodstock, just to the south of Pomfret. Woodstock was a natural choice for newcomers as it was an old, well-preserved village hosting the county seat with a population intellectually inclined, surrounded by a plethora of old farms in the surrounding area.[4]

One of the best ways to see the extent to which newcomers came to Woodstock and the region near Joe Ranger's neighborhood is to examine the various "society" maps published of the area. These maps informed newcomers who else of their class had bought old farmhouses in the area and where they were located.

One of these first society maps dates from 1934 and shows the town of Woodstock as a center of gentrification. It also shows that just over the northern town line in Pomfret and Barnard, and to the west in Bridgewater, several former farms had been recently settled by newcomers. The expansion of Greater Woodstock had begun. Over the next decade more people came from out of state to buy property near Woodstock and a map from 1949 shows the progression new-comers were making into the secluded spots in these outlying towns. By the time Doug Ross put out his map in 1965, Quechee, Hartland, and Reading were also included, showing that most of the society people who had come to the Woodstock area by that time actually owned homes outside of Woodstock.5

Pomfret became especially popular with newcomers seeking rural residences near Woodstock. An examination of the transfer of farms and old houses from natives to newcomers between 1920 and 1990 shows when each house became gentrified. In the 1920s, only two former farms in North Pomfret were bought and transformed by "summer people." After *Rural Vermont* was published, twelve more old places were bought in the 1930s. The decade of the 1940s found eleven and the 1950s, seven, as better automobiles enabled easier commuting to North Pomfret. During the 1960s, an explosion of interest in all things Vermont resulted in nineteen old houses chang-ing hands to people from elsewhere. The 1970s and 1980s saw less buying, as only ten properties were gentrified during those two decades, but this decline occurred because there was an ever shrink-ing pool of old farms for sale. By 1990, 77% of North Pomfret's for-mer farm and village houses had been gentrified.6

After coming to rural Vermont, some newcomers wrote about their experiences in their adopted home. A plethora of books about coming to Vermont and interacting with its people appeared between the 1930s and 1960s. Some positive attention was paid to Vermont because of a perception that the state had toughed it out through the

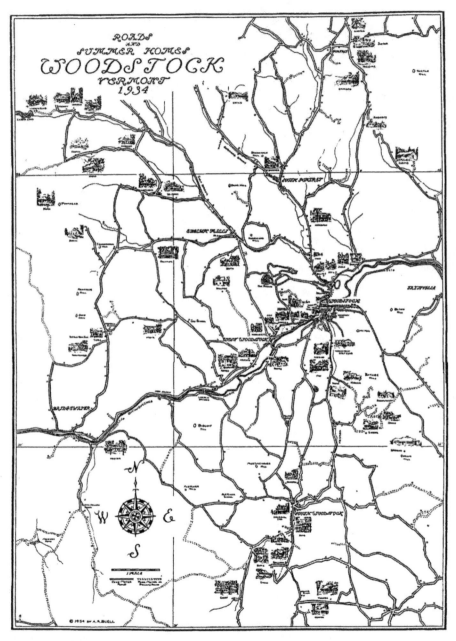

A.S. Buel's society map of greater Woodstock, Vermont 1934.
Courtesy of the Woodstock Historical Society.

Great Depression, a reaffirmation of Vermonters' image as hardy and self-reliant. Such positive perceptions were enhanced by the state's local town meeting democracy, during the years of fighting fascism in Europe. Vermont was an example to hold up as a vital part of American democracy and its benefits to mankind. As a result, columnists and authors came to the state to learn what they could about the character of Vermont. While doing so, they also learned about Vermont characters.

The negative image of rural Vermont in popular literature ended in the 1930s with the onset of the Great Depression. For a change, the nation as a whole got a taste of the hard times Vermont had been dealing with for decades, and as a result, attitudes about rural Vermont and Vermonters began to change. While it was true that Vermont had been portrayed in the popular press as a good place to get away from, it now seemed Vermont might have something to teach the rest of the nation about getting by in tough economic times. In a March 1932 article for *Harper's* magazine, author Bernard DeVoto, who later became famous for his histories of the American West, noted the changing perception of rural New England by comparing it to the rest of the nation sunk deep in the Depression.[7] What was going on in the nation had been the way of life in New England for some time, DeVoto pointed out. While business activity in the nation "was sick...New England business...wasn't quite so sick." Panic had "possessed America, but New England wasn't quite so scared." It seemed the current hard time "wasn't quite so bad in New England, despair wasn't quite so ghastly." Indeed, DeVoto wrote, how "should hard times terrify New England? It had had hard times for sixty years" and had found "a way to endure a perpetual depression."[8]

In laying out how rural New Englanders got by, DeVoto highlighted the lifestyle of "Jason" and his wife "Emma," Vermonters who DeVoto knew from vacationing in the state. First of all, they worked with what they already had available to them. Jason had piled evergreen boughs around his house so the falling snow would cover them and "make them an insulation that would be expensive in the city." The logs outside the house would be turned into "fuel that Jason burns all year round." Emma had a garden and she kept her "potatoes, cabbages, and beets" in a pit under the floor of one of their sheds and "filled her pantry with jars of home-grown corn, string beans, carrots, and a little fruit." Once when DeVoto had stopped by, he found Emma "making bread and doughnuts" for dinner along with vegetables and "a rabbit stew."

The couple farmed "about seventy acres of hillside" land on which they pastured their small herd of cows and made maple syrup and sugar, which brought in "about one half of" the four hundred dollars "that Jason handles in a year." "On such an income," DeVoto explained, which was "less than a fifth of what [the] Department of Commerce estimated to be the minimum capable of supporting an American family, Jason has brought up his children in health, comfort, and contentment."[9]

"There are thousands like Jason [and Emma] on the hillside farms of Vermont," declared DeVoto. They "have never thrown themselves upon the charity of the nation. They have never assaulted Congress, demanding a place at the national trough." They have "clung" to their land with solvency, "righteousness," and independent "pride." Yet somehow, "out of nothing at all," with "natural resources the poorest in the Union, with an economic system incapable of exploitation, in a geography and climate that make necessary for survival the very extreme of effort," they carry on. The "district nurse makes her rounds, the town roads are hard. The white schoolhouse sends it products to...high school and on to the university. The inspector calls and tests the family cow [for disease]." The "State bul-

letins reach the mailbox at the corner. The crippled and superannu-
ated are secure. If [someone] falls ill he will be cared for...[and] if his
crop fails his neighbors will find food for his family." Vermont was
heaven on earth. "I cannot imagine," DeVoto concluded, "a perfect-
ed state that could improve upon it."[10]

The reason why Vermonters were doing all right during the
Depression, DeVoto declared, was because they were tenacious and
thrifty. "Hell! [DeVoto's Jason] couldn't remember any times that
hadn't been hard." There was nothing "to do though, but pull up
your belt and hang on." The buffalo coat he wore was "in its third
generation in his family." Emma's rag rugs are "made from garments
whose other usefulness was ended....The pans above her sink date
from no ascertainable period; she and her daughters will use them a
long time yet." Jason's rocking chair has been "patched and var-
nished" and Emma "has renewed its cushions innumerable times.
The trademark on Jason's wagon is that of a factory which has not
existed for forty years." He "does not know how many shafts he has
made for it; he has patched the bed, bent iron for the running gear,
set new tires on the wheels perhaps ten times. Now he contemplates
putting the bed and shafts on the frame of an old Ford and will move
his loads on rubber tires."[11]

Is this a "squalid picture," DeVoto asked his readers, "a summa-
ry of penny-pinching poverty that degrades the human spirit?" No,
he answered, not "unless you have been victimized by what has never
deluded Jason" and other Vermonters: Things "are something which
are to be used; they are not the measure of happiness and success."

This was the distilled Yankee wisdom that DeVoto was trying to
impress upon his readers. The "Yankee has experienced nothing but
what he was taught to expect. Out of this wisdom, in his frigid climate, against the resistance of his granite fields," he made what he
has. Yankee values have served Vermonters well, concluded DeVoto,

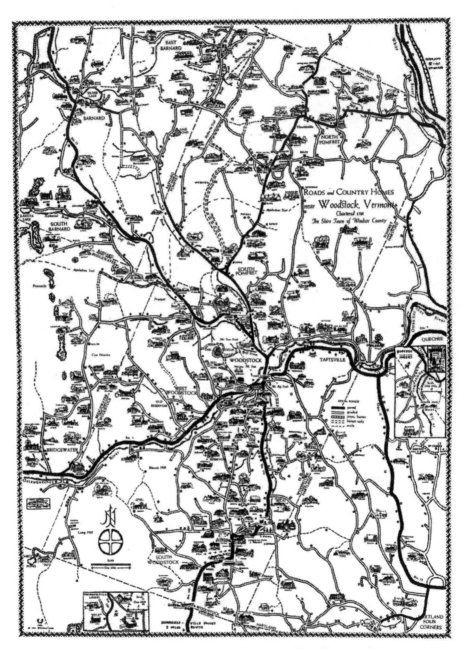

Douglas Ross's society map of greater Woodstock 1965.
Courtesy of the Woodstock Historical Society.

and perhaps the rest of the country could learn from them.[12]

Another example reflecting the changing attitudes about rural Vermont was Walter and Margaret Hard's *This is Vermont*.[13] Published in 1936, their book highlighted Vermonters' conservative values as an example for the rest of the nation to embrace during the economic hard times. While acknowledging the challenges facing rural Vermont and the eugenic nature of efforts at improvement up to that time, the Hards also expressed a different attitude. They accepted and celebrated Vermont and Vermonters. With firsthand anecdotes of their own travels and experiences in the state the Hards sowed the seeds that later grew into a flowering of literature about Vermont and Vermonters.

This is Vermont is a sort of tour of the state, region by region, with the Hards as guides highlighting the local attractions and culture. Previous "motor guides" to the state included much about roads, scenery, and accommodations, but nothing about Vermonters themselves. The Hards' book changed this formula. Their survey of fellow Vermonters was both descriptive and imaginative.[14]

In one passage describing having car trouble, the Hards also described the people they met, including the local storekeeper and mechanic, but also a neighboring farmer who took the couple in for the night until their car was fixed. The farmer they described simply as "tall" and "pleasant-faced," but also as "resourceful." Resourcefulness was a trait the Hards were eager to ascribe to these rural Vermonters in the depth of the Great Depression. Talking between themselves, the Hards noted that "These people know how to live carefully and plainly, and yet get a lot of satisfaction out of life." They gave off "the impression of not being afraid of anything, especially of not being afraid to live with fugality." The Hards then suggested that this characteristic was prevalent because Vermonters have "been used to it for generations" because they had been in a state of economic depression for so long. And even though most Vermonters did not live in dire need, they "haven't forgotten that age-old habit of thrift and moderation." Rural Vermonters were put in a positive light against the bleak background of the past.[15]

Several other interactions with "native" Vermonters led the Hards to some of the same conclusions about the state and its people as Bernard DeVoto. Although the state was backward in many ways, that was alright. After talking about the speed of driving, Margaret Hard declared that she liked to drive at her own speed. Walter then observed, "Probably that is why Vermonters are usually individualists. They've been used to going along on their own back roads at their own gait" with nobody to disturb them for so long. Time wasn't money here. "I have an idea," Hard continued, "that's why country men often seem lazy to the hustling business man. Their time isn't bought or sold." Vermonters weren't lazy, they had their own pace of life.[16]

Toward the end of the book, the Hards again took up the character of Vermonters after an encounter with one "enthusiastic native" who had told them about Hazen's Notch. Upon leaving, Margaret asked her husband his thoughts about "that old fellow at the filling station" they had just talked to. "He wasn't grammatical, and he certainly didn't care how he looked," she observed, "but he was a gentleman and his attitude toward this region was almost religious." After considering, Walter responded that in some ways Vermonters are "modern," driving automobiles and adapting to new ways, but in other ways they are "just like their grandfathers.... They aren't stampeded or herded and they aren't unhappy because they can't have everything." During the Hards' tour of Vermont, they had learned that the decades of hard times and decline had actually improved Vermonters by creating habits of frugality, patience, and resourcefulness, and they were eager to tell everyone about it. This was just what

they thought the country needed to hear in 1936: Vermont and
Vermonters were an example to follow.[17]

Subsequent publications by newcomers to Vermont followed the
lead taken by DeVoto and the Hards in including descriptions of
encounters with "Vermonters." In 1941 Henry Lent's *Sixty Acres More
or Less* introduced readers to his family's experience in buying an old
farm in Newfane, and a Vermonter they encountered along the way.
Lent, his wife, and two sons lived in Connecticut near enough to New
York City so Lent could commute to work. The Lents also rented a
small farm, but couldn't afford to buy it.

One day after having lunch with an associate whose cousin "had
just bought an old abandoned farm in Vermont," Lent wrote for the
State booklet *Vermont Farms for Sale*. After perusing it, the family took
a trip to Vermont to see if they could find a place to buy for themselves. On the way to one of the places listed in the booklet they got
lost. The vignette of losing their way and asking for directions provided an opportunity, and a vehicle, for Lent to introduce his readers
to one type of Vermonter: the reticent character.[18]

The Lents had gone farther than they thought they should and
decided to stop at a "weather-beaten unpainted house" with "an old
bony horse standing disconsolately" in the pasture in order to "find
out where" they were. Henry Lent left his wife in the car and made
his way to the house. When he "knocked on the door there was no
response." After knocking again, he heard "a shuffling noise" coming from the inside and then "the door swung slowly open." There
in front of him "stood a kindly, gnomelike little old man" dressed in
"a long black overcoat, felt boots, and a deerstalker cap" that shield-
ed his "shaggy white brows."[19]

Lent greeted the fellow with a "How do you do?...very politely,"
but the old man didn't answer and just stood there looking at him.
Thinking he might be deaf, Lent repeated himself in a loud voice.

"Still no answer. Somewhat baffled, and also somewhat desperate," Lent said, "I think we're lost on your mountain. Do you know where the Sherwood's place is?" To his "intense relief" the old man "quietly uttered the two words, 'I do.' *Period.*" Thinking it "some sort of game" Lent had "never heard of," he then figured it was his turn and asked if the fellow could tell him "how to get there." "Once again," the fellow "blinked his eyes and uttered two words, 'I can.' *Period.*" Thinking of Poe's raven, Lent knew he should ask another question. This time he asked the man if he would mind telling Lent "how to get there please?" With that, the old fellow stepped out onto the porch and "pointed down the road in the direction from which" Lent "had just come." "If you're looking for the Sherwoods' you might go back beyond the bend in the road and find a mailbox with their name on it, about a mile" away. Lent then protested that he had "just passed by there" and "didn't see any mailbox." "Can't help that. It's there," replied the man. As Lent tried to thank him, the man turned to go back into the house, but Lent had another question. Does "this road come out anywhere if we keep going?" The old man turned slowly and said, "Matter of two miles, you might say."[20]

Back at the car, Lent told his wife of his encounter with "Herman the Hermit" and that the place was back where they had just come from. After retracing their route, they found the mailbox set back off the road in "the bushes" and thus, the place they were looking for. After looking around, they decided to continue on past the old man's house to see where they came out. As they drove by, they spied the old man "sitting on his porch." The Lents waved to him, "but," he "gave no sign that he had seen" them. In the final analysis, Henry Lent declared, "it takes more than a wave of the hand" to win over a Vermonter like "*him*."[21]

Elliott Merrick's *Green Mountain Farm* published in 1948, expanded on Lent's introduction of independent Vermont characters.

Written for those who "long for warmth and simplicity in the midst of today's complexity," the book "tells of country life as it appears to" Merrick the writer/poet/explorer. Filling the pages, Merrick "writes of his need for the simple life, of his love for his wife and family, [and] his affection for the oddities of his neighbors." Elliott Merrick taught his readers that the oddities of his rural Vermont neighbors were endearing.[22]

Within the first seven pages of his book, Merrick informed his readers that Vermont "was full of local character." In fact, there "were more odd fantastic characters per square foot" in his town "than any other." While the "region was full of heartening eccentrics," Merrick admitted that "it took a long time to know and appreciate them." Part of his own success in getting to know these people, he guessed, was "that we were immediately considered a bit peculiar ourselves" by the locals. Neighbors wondered why educated people like the Merricks would come to their poor community and choose to live the hard existence they themselves experienced out of necessity. Perhaps, Merrick mused, the fact that he was considered odd "gave us something of an entrée into the charmed inner circle" of the local characters.[23]

Merrick delighted in telling stories about his neighborly characters. There was Ted Norris, the Tanner's "hired man" who had been a Harvard graduate, but when Merrick met him, he was "a grizzled short-thick man who seldom spoke, even to children." Norris had once owned a farm and was noted for his "fine team of black horses," but later he began to "drink himself senseless." It was a "well established routine" for him to come to town, drink, get drunk, and then let the horses take him home as he lay wasted in his wagon. Merrick speculated that old Norris would still be continuing that routine "except that Ted Norris lost his farm and his team too and hardly made enough now to keep himself in tobacco and overalls."

Thanks to Merrick, rural Vermont drunks like Norris could be looked at with a bit of acceptance and humor instead of loathing.[24]

Merrick also wrote about his neighbor, Chester. Chester was a carpenter whose "thin shoulders and scrawny whiskers imparted a deceptive quality of fragility." Merrick hired Chester to help shingle his roof one April. Taking Chester's judgment that "the weather would hold fair" for a few days, the pair commenced stripping the house of its old roofing.[25]

Chester quickly won Merrick's respect. When they had it stripped "Chester climbed up on the roof and laid on shingles like mad." As they worked, Merrick wondered at the "shelf of a couple of boards supported by several shingle-bundle battens tacked with shingle nails to the roof" which Chester had arranged for the pair to work on. Perhaps sensing Merrick's initial apprehension, Chester reassured him that if "one brace gives, the other'll hold – probably."

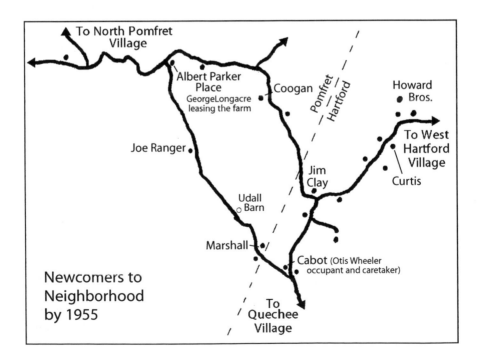

In the same breath Chester "claimed he was frightened of heights" and recounted an accident he had once involving a ladder, accounting for how he got his "lame leg." [26]

Although uncertain at first, Merrick worked with "Chester on the roof" and "began a long process of watching and working and learning that lasted for years." Chester taught him that "most jobs in building and fixing are not magic, but can be managed by trying and looking and using common sense." Common sense. Another value Merrick found his Vermont neighbors possessed.[27]

If common sense reigned in Vermont, so did provincialism. That was a plus, however. Indeed, Merrick felt Vermonters epitomized the simple life without the corrupting influences of the outside world. His visit with "Zak" one "sloppy, sleety afternoon" as they "sat by the stove" revealed that the biggest place Zak had ever been was Sherbrooke, Quebec. "That Sherbrooke is a big place I want to tell you," related Zak. The buildings there "are so thick and high the sun never strikes." Informing Merrick that one can "get lost" there easily, Zak said that he was there once and "nightfall come on and I was caught there with no way to get home." Having to get a hotel room, Zak tried to dazzle Merrick with the information that he had slept "seven storeys up!" adding that he "Slept real well, too." In Zak, Merrick found a local who marveled at things most people took for granted.[28]

Another character Merrick wrote about was a fellow who helped him cut ice one day. This man was "on the town." He also had a wooden leg. Merrick described him as someone "who works very hard, but cannot get a start or a place of his own." "He works much harder than I do," Merrick continued, "but he cannot make a living." Describing sawing the blocks of ice for his ice house, Merrick then marveled at the ingenuity of this fellow, who had made his own ice saw "out of an old drag-saw" and which was "better than my bought one." Although the fellow "had no mittens," just a pair of worn-out "heavy leather gloves with no lining, he never complained." Merrick meditated on why it was that there were people with nothing who "carry most of the world's burdens." "Oh well," he concluded, "it has always been so and it will always be so." Besides, he mused, "Pegleg might be worse off if he were a successful Junior Executive with a starched collar and an ulcer." Imagining his sawing companion that night, Merrick reflected that he "will be home, sawing tomorrow's firewood with a bucksaw" by the light of the moon, and that he probably "will be glad of the moonlight because it saves him burning oil in his lantern." Yankee characters do not complain about their lot in Merrick's Vermont neighborhood, they live with what they have.[29]

Rounding off his litany of characters, Merrick included "Ethan Cutler" who was "as solid as his name." Living in the nearby town of Albany, Cutler was "full of tales of local lore, an ardent hunter" and "an ingenious Yankee when it came to working in wood or metal." Through Elliott Merrick's work, readers became familiarized with rural Vermont characters, epitomized by Cutter and the rest of the cast, and Merrick's success in interacting with them.[30] A few years later a book appeared that highlighted the practicalities of successful interaction with rural Vermonters.

Like Elliott Merrick's *Green Mountain Farm*, Elsie and John Masterson's *Nothing Whatever To Do* tells of their own experience in moving to Vermont.[31] Published in 1956, the Mastersons' book included local characters and their interactions, but it went further than that. It showed current and prospective newcomers that with patience and understanding, they themselves could be accepted into the Vermonters' community.

Elsie Masterson admitted that when she first moved to "Goshen," she thought her neighbors "were bound to be nice, simple people living on rolling farms, four or five miles in one direction or another."

She never guessed that she would be judged by these people. Her neighbor "Uncle Rob" assured her, however. "Don't you worry none, girl," he told her, "They'll like ye. Wait'll they know ye like I do. They'll like ye." Somewhat taken aback by this comment she asked, "Why shouldn't they? You sound as if they shouldn't." Slowly, and with individual acts, she found the acceptance she sought. Being an ambitious woman, "word got around" that she was a "worker." "Higher praise," she wrote, "could be given no Vermont woman."[32]

Even though she found acceptance, Elsie Masterson also found she had to adjust to the social constraints of the community. "These were the social mores of the town of Goshen, I discovered. The men were with the men. The women were with the women. Never did I pass a word with any male member of the population at any town gathering, meeting, or church service."[33]

Along with gender divisions, she found herself initially irked by her neighbors who kept coming over to borrow items from her and her husband. Wondering why they didn't just buy their own tools, she later realized that "these borrowers, were simply laying the foundation for a friendship that meant we could call on them any time, any time at all.... After a while, John did ask them to return the things they had borrowed by such and such a day, and this they did not mind. They all knew they could come borrow them again. Any time."[34]

One of the borrowers Masterson wrote about was Zeke Thayer. "Zeke was an anomaly. On the surface he seemed a country bumpkin. Notwithstanding, he was a shrewd and a clever fellow; a kind and sympathetic friend; a man to trust, but not in a trade for anything, because he loved nothing better than to trade you down." The Mastersons had already learned about getting the bad end of a trade with Zeke. One day, Zeke showed up wanting to acquire on old garage the Mastersons had on their property. He had an old building he didn't need, and knowing the Mastersons were looking for some lumber for a new building project, Zeke proposed they swap buildings even. Answering before thinking, John Masterson agreed. Later on he found it more work than it was worth taking Zeke's building apart for the old lumber, while Zeke had moved the garage to his own place in one piece. Mrs. Masterson concluded that Zeke's "toothless grin belied his very sharp Vermont acumen." One had to accept being taken in once and a while by these Vermonters.[35]

Masterson's most important lesson for readers planning to move to Vermont and getting along with the locals was that it was possible to care about these people. She singled out "Uncle Rob" as an example. "Here and there was a Vermonter like him. Call him 'hired man,' call him 'friend,' call him 'mentor,' what you will, but a Vermonter he truly was, and from him we viewed them all - all the Vermonters we ever knew - in a light of understanding and gratitude. He was there when I arrived. How John got him, I never... actually knew. But Uncle Rob was there, slightly suspicious of me, withdrawn, nonetheless gallant."[36]

When Uncle Rob died, the Mastersons found "it was strange and lost and wrong without him; our loss of Uncle Rob was an intimate, a family thing. We spent days talking of him, weeping for him, and remembering his stalwart help in John's building of the ski area, his championship of me, always, always, his gossiping in our kitchen, his appreciation of all that was beautiful, his pride at his political acumen, at his past prominence as Representative of the Town of Goshen at the Legislature, his gentility, his distaste over the Chair Case, his love of Lucinda, of John, of Blueberry Hill. He was a very fine fellow, this Uncle Rob. This Vermonter."[37]

The Mastersons' Uncle Rob was a special fellow. A Vermonter. This theme was kept up in subsequent publications. Increasingly, the popular image of a Vermonter became one of an old man. Judd Hale, the former editor-in-chief of *Yankee* magazine, declared that after he began working for *Yankee* in the late 1950s, he learned about "real Yankees." A true Yankee, he said, "was male, *never* young, lived in either Maine or Vermont, was not wealthy [and] not well educated, but very smart." Hale's popular magazine promoted this male Yankee image for decades and helped spread interest in Vermonters, their culture, and their humor.[38]

One of the men appearing in *Yankee* over the years was Dartmouth History Professor Allen Foley, one of the great promoters of Vermont's "old timers," in a 1957 article focusing on their humor and wit. Foley's stories about Vermonters buttressed Hale's assessment that in the popular imagination, a Vermonter was an old, reticent, weathered, farmer: a man, an "Old Timer." The tales Foley told and wrote about his neighbors and other old Vermont men he encountered, along with secondhand accounts of Vermont characters, helped set the stage for an extended celebration of old men.[39]

Born in Massachusetts, Foley went through the Framingham public schools before earning a BA at Dartmouth and eventually a doctorate at Harvard. Coming back to Dartmouth to teach in 1929, Foley became legendary on campus for his American History course entitled "Western Expansion," popularly nicknamed "Cowboys and Indians," which he taught until his retirement in 1964. He also became legendary off campus as the man who wrote *What the Old Timer Said.*[40]

What the Old Timer Said was the culmination of years of interest in Vermont and Vermont humor. Initially Foley was interested in New England history and the public talks he later became famous for originally focused on history and not Vermont humor. At a presentation he gave to the Woodstock Historical Society in the spring of 1946 he gave an "interesting survey of pioneer life in New England, tracing the flow of population to Vermont, and later westward." While "interesting," this talk was probably not very "engaging."[41]

To liven up his history lectures, Foley began integrating "North Country Humor" into his talks. His audiences, including "women's clubs, Rotary Clubs, Lions Clubs, community dinners and other groups in practically every city and hamlet in New Hampshire and Vermont" reacted favorably to his new focus.

Having moved to Norwich, Vermont, at the time the state was growing popular in the public mind after World War II, Foley switched his historical and North Country talks to presentations about "Vermont Humor" and began speaking to groups outside of northern New England eager to hear about witty Vermonters.

A sampling of Foley's presentations throughout the years include the Worcester (Massachusetts) Rotary Club in October 1949, the Beverly (Massachusetts) Teacher's Association in May, 1950 the fourth program of the 1952-1953 Town Hall series at the Rensselaer Polytechnic Institute in Troy, New York, the annual George

Allen R. Foley, Dartmouth professor and promoter of Yankee humor. From Allen R. Foley, What the Old-Timer Said.

Washington birthday breakfast at the Passaic, New Jersey First Presbyterian Church in February 1956, the Waterbury (Connecticut) Kiwanis Club in June 1959, and an October 1963 presentation to the student body at Babson Institute in Wellesley, Massachusetts.[42]

Foley's talks were written about in the local papers wherever he appeared. His talk at Babson Institute made four Massachusetts newspapers between September 30 and October 6, 1963. *The Needham Times, Framingham News, Wellesley Townsman,* and *Boston Globe* together reached almost half a million readers in the course of a week, informing them that Foley's talk on Vermont humor would be "free and open to the public." Even those who had never heard of Foley, did not know that Vermonters were especially humorous, or did not attend the lecture, had a seed planted in their mind that there may be something special about Vermont, just the same.[43]

It is not surprising that many of those hearing Foley's Vermont humor talks encouraged him to publish them as a book. It didn't take much prodding to get Foley interested. After some years of false starts, he eventually published *What the Old-Timer Said* with the Stephen Greene Press in Brattleboro, Vermont, in June 1971. It became a hit and Foley put out another book of more Vermont humor four years later entitled *The Old-Timer Talks Back*. A third collection was in the works when Foley died at the age of 79 on February 16, 1978.[44]

Some of Allen Foley's characters were his Norwich neighbors. Charlie Hodgdon, the town road agent, fed Foley stories and brothers Paul and Fred Metcalf, who lived up on Dutton Hill, provided sage advice and also appeared several times in Foleys first book with dry, witty, one-liners. Dorrance Sargent, "tenth-generation American and third-generation son of Norwich," provided Foley with one of his "most rewarding friendships," and many stories. The first eight pages of *What the Old-Timer Said* is devoted exclusively to Dorrance. Sargent was a "good old-fashioned Vermonter - and a 'character' to boot," and "one of those folks whose rate of change was very slow. One could glimpse in him, it seemed, a living picture of older days and ways." If he had wanted to, Foley probably could have written his books exlusively with the stories from Norwich without depending on any others from around the state.[45]

Along with his Norwich neighbors, Foley may have used some of the stories he heard in Pomfret, for he had become very familiar with the town and its people. A former Pomfret native who was working on a farm in Hartford in the early 1930s related in letters home when Professor Foley had visited and continued on to Pomfret with the farm's owners. Many of Foley's trips to Pomfret were to fill in for the minister at the Pomfret Congregational Church. During the first half of the 1900s, students and professors from Dartmouth helped out the surrounding town's small community churches by filling in for those whose ministers had quit, were ill, or were non-existent.[46]

Charlotte Warren Harvey remembers Foley preaching the Sunday service many times at the North Pomfret church and having dinner with her family afterwards, as they "were great ones...to entertain the minister." Her father, Bill Warren, epitomized the classic Vermonter with his manners and stories. While Harvard educated and a scholar of ancient languages, Warren was also a farmer, Pomfret native, and guest-house owner who could pour on the down-home stereotype of Yankee humor whenever it was warranted. Charlotte recalled the times Allen Foley and her father sat together after dinner, swapping Old-Timer stories. Even though it isn't known if any of Warren's stories included Joe Ranger or if any made it into Foley's repertoire, the interactions Foley had with people like Warren helped him formulate his image of the Vermont Yankee character as a witty old man.[47] In such an atmosphere it is easy to understand how someone like Joe Ranger could get caught up in the hype and earn his own spot in the public imagination as a local Vermont character.

8

Encounters

Many newcomers came to Vermont, and eventually met and befriended local natives like Joe Ranger. After settling in, newcomers to Pomfret quickly learned about Joe in particular. Some heard about him before they saw him. One woman claimed that when she first came to Pomfret, Joe Ranger was one of the first things her new neighbors told her about.[1]

When out-of-staters came to the area and bought property, they inevitably became part of the neighborhood. Although from different backgrounds with different attitudes and expectations about rural life, these newcomers formed relationships with the natives living nearby. Some avoided unnecessary contact with their rural neighbors. They had come to Vermont for the quiet and to not be bothered. Their interactions with their neighbors were strictly utilitarian. When they needed unskilled labor, they hired those living nearby. Springs of water had to be dug out, water lines located, fields mowed. Natives provided the labor that helped maintain a pastoral ideal.[2]

Elder members of the Andrew Marshall family fit into the category of newcomers who shunned unnecessary contact with their native neighbors. Andrew Marshall, Sr. had purchased the old Brockway farm in 1937 and enjoyed his rural retreat particularly because he could regulate his social contacts. While he invited guests from his own social circle in Boston to come to his summer home, native folks were not among the invited guests. Instead, his contact with locals was out of necessity.

Otis Wheeler was one native the Marshalls depended on. Wheeler had worked for Alice Wood for years, living in the house with her. When she sold the farm to the Cabot family as a summer home, Otis was included in the bargain. The Cabots needed someone to take care of the place. Otis worked for the family by keeping the farm going and maintaining the pastoral idyll the Cabots sought. Like the Cabots, the Marshalls found they also needed Otis Wheeler occasionally. It is not clear how much Otis worked for Andrew Marshall, Sr., but he proved essential for Marshall's son and daughter-in-law, Malcolm and Andy.

Although the elder Marshall did not seek out local connections, he could not help but notice Joe Ranger. Given Joe's frequent treks down to West Hartford by foot, an encounter was just a matter of time. Although we don't know the details of their first encounter, it is easy to envision Joe coming down the road as Mr. Marshall was out in his garden or out on his lawn. He probably had heard about Joe through Otis, so he easily recognized him. No doubt, Joe was the first to speak. He probably stopped, standing in the road while he talked. Mr. Marshall would have been polite and would have responded to Joe, even perhaps, inquiring into his life in the area. That would have been about it. Joe would have walked on and the newcomer would have gone back to his endeavors. More than likely, Andrew Marshall, Sr. encountered Joe other times, but it is doubtful he went up to see him or sought his company. In the Marshalls' case, it was not this older generation that sought out Joe. They were interested in their country homes and social circles. Instead, it was the children and grandchildren of Andrew and Jessie Marshall who became enamored with Joe Ranger.

The younger generation of Marshalls not only enjoyed spending time at their parents country homes, they also found themselves becoming interested in the surrounding area and its people. The younger folks had always come to their parents' Vermont summer homes. For "years and years" the families of Andrew Jr., Malcolm, Jessie, and Blanche Marshall came. Starting out as visits to see their parents, these trips quickly expanded to include walks around the back roads of North Pomfret and West Hartford, dips in the White River, stops at the local store, and conversations with the natives.[3]

Malcolm Marshall and his wife Andy took an especial interest in his parents' Vermont home. By the 1950s, Malcolm's parents only spent about a month in the summer at the old Brockway place. Andrew and Jessie Marshall were getting older and sought easier accommodations back home in Newton, Massachusetts for most of the summer. Their retreat back down country gave Malcolm and Andy an opportunity to bring their children to the Vermont house without worrying about imposing on his parents.

Malcolm's siblings also took advantage of the Vermont house for short vacations, but Malcolm became the family's steward of the place. He spent the most time there. Malcolm Marshall changed the trajectory of his life when in his prime he gave up a successful banking career to take up teaching. One outcome of this change was that he now had the summers off. As a result, he and Andy and their children made the old farm their summer home.

Spending the whole summer in Vermont gave the Marshalls ample opportunity to get to know their neighbors. Otis Wheeler had done the occasional job for Malcolm's parents, but under Malcolm and Andy's stewardship, Otis became their man Friday. Otis plowed the garden, dug out their spring, did light repairs, opened up the house when the family came, closed it up after they left, and checked on it while they were gone. He would cruise the road looking over their fields and stop in daily at the house to make sure it hadn't been broken into. Otis Wheeler was the Marshalls' most important local connection. Even while they were in Vermont, the family relied on Otis, and as a result, they got to know him pretty well.

Otis Wheeler's natural stubbornness shown through for the Marshalls, and they reveled in it. He would always do a job for them *his way*. Malcolm loved gardening and relied on Otis to plow up the garden spot each spring. Malcolm gave much thought to his gardens and had specific plans for their layout, including the initial plowing. He would ask Otis to come up and plow and then watch for Otis to come so he could supervise and direct. When Otis showed up Malcolm would point out where the garden was to be and tell him how he wanted it plowed. Otis would nod his head and not say a word. Then he would begin plowing, his way. Malcolm would see Otis doing just the opposite of what he wanted and he would yell and wave his arms for Otis to stop. Otis would stop the tractor and, turning his ear toward Malcolm say "haaar." Malcolm would stride over and give Otis the instructions again. Otis would nod. Malcolm stepped back out of the way and Otis would continue plowing the same as before. Otis Wheeler "wasn't going to change his way for anybody."[4]

Along with Otis, the Marshalls also got to know the Howards. Neither family ever visited each other's house, but they would usually chat by the road if the Howards stopped on their way to the heifer barn at the Udall place. Ernest and Ralph would talk with Malcolm. They would stay in their vehicle and talk out the open window. Malcolm certainly sought the Howards' views on gardening matters as well as local news. But Andy didn't get to know the Howards. She wasn't given the opportunity. If the men were out by the road talking and she came out, Ernest and Ralph left. She remembered several times making a beeline for their vehicle and their driving off without a word. She thought it strange. But strange as it may have seemed to Andy Marshall, it made perfect sense to the local men. The men in the neighborhood weren't used to confronting a talkative, outgoing woman with an English accent. They were scared of her. Even Otis Wheeler was a little leery. He succinctly reflected common local male opinion of Andy when he described her as "a fancy-talking foreigner."[5]

Andy Marshall did find one man in the neighborhood who wasn't afraid of her, however: Joe Ranger. Andy no doubt had heard of Joe from her in-laws and Otis Wheeler, and most likely it didn't take long for her to meet him. Once Andy and Malcolm began coming up to the house summers, she explored the neighborhood by foot. She traveled the Quechee-West Hartford road, up the Town Farm road in Hartford, up past Jim Clay's to Bunker Hill, and up past her place toward Joe Ranger's place.

While walking, Andy took in the natural surroundings. Flowers were an especial delight. With her little kids in tow, she would examine the sides of the roads looking for whatever specimens caught her fancy. For their part, the children more than likely took to the things that crawled or jumped. In Joe, mother and children both made a special find.

Many years later, Andy Marshall tried to remember if she first met Joe Ranger while exploring the "lower lands" along the stream and pond near his house, or if she met him while walking on the road. It doesn't matter. What she does remember is that this little man with a "sqeaky voice" was "immensely friendly." Evidently she had heard that Joe lived alone and was somewhat of a recluse. What a surprise it was for her to find him talkative and very "interested in what you were doing." Being something of a naturalist, she was doubly excited to learn that Joe knew much about the habits of the birds and animals native to the area. In addition to learning more about the local flora and fauna, Andy also discovered that Joe was a character.

Joe fit the local stories. He walked everywhere, was dirty, stank of liquor, and was witty. Every time he walked down by the Marshalls' house, he was carrying a stick with a bag tied on the end. If he was spotted by the Marshall children, out of the house they would bound, in stocking feet or what have you.

The Marshall kids just loved Joe. It's not hard to see why. He paid attention to them, always spoke with them. Andy remembers Joe patting their heads and hands as he talked. The stories he told also enthralled the children. One favorite involved a fox picking a fight with a beaver resulting in the beaver getting the better of the fox.

The Marshall children were fascinated by Joe and part of their fascination had to do with his living conditions. One of them asked him how he kept warm in the winter. Joe said that he slept with his cow. When questioned if he and the cow really did sleep together Joe replied, "Sure we do, we keep each other warm." Andy Marshall still isn't sure if Joe was kidding.

One time when Andy and the kids were driving up past Joe's, they saw him outside. Immediately, the car windows rolled down. "Hi Joe, hi Joe," they yelled. He came over to see them and ended up inviting them all inside his house. This was the first time any of them had ever been inside and Andy wasn't sure what to expect. She had "never, never seen such a place in my life," she remembered over forty years later. While Andy was shocked, she didn't say anything about the mess to Joe. Her kids did, however. Her oldest son, Duncan, came right out and asked, "Don't you ever clean up?" Without batting an eye Joe replied, "What for?" "That was exactly what Joe Ranger said," Andy recalled. "And," she added, "This was to [my] kids the dream of heaven: never clean up, never do anything, just be there, learn as you wanted." Joe Ranger had made his mark on the Marshall family.[6]

Although not as gregarious as the Marshalls, the Coogans eventually met Joe and formed their own narrative of him. After coming up from Boston and buying the old Wheeler place where Otis had grown up, Peter Coogan decided he was going to raise beef cattle. The results were disastrous. While family members talk in general about their father's misadventure with cattle, the details are spelled out by a neighbor. Dennis Clay remembers being a young fellow when the Coogans began coming to Vermont. The Clay farm was at the foot of the hill from the old Wheeler place. Thus, every time the Coogans came or went they had to pass by. Eventually, Peter and Barbara met Jim Clay.

On one of their stops, Peter told Jim about his plans for raising beef cattle. Jim was a native dairy farmer struggling along and was incredulous about Coogan's plans. He told Peter Coogan what he thought. Coogan replied that he had been raised on a midwestern farm and knew what he was doing. He was going to show Jim "how to make money without beating your brains out."[7]

The Coogans stocked their "farm" with beef cattle and during the summer all went well. The cattle stayed in the pasture and ate grass. During this time the family kept up the fences and saw that a large amount of hay was put in the barn for winter feed. This was all right. The family could come and go as they pleased and the cattle took care of themselves. Come winter, however, the family would be back in Massachusetts. The plan was to hire George Longacre, who lived on Albert Parker's place after Albert moved down to North Pomfret Village, to feed the cattle morning and night, see that they had water, and make sure that all was well. This plan started out fine, but ended in disaster. One family member put it succinctly when she said that Longacre ended up selling their hay and starving the cattle. It became obvious that if one couldn't be on site to oversee the care of the cattle, it wasn't going to work. This was a bitter pill for Peter Coogan to swallow, but he gained the respect of Jim Clay when he later admitted to Clay that he "had lost his shirt" in the fiasco.[8]

This misadventure with raising cattle precluded the Coogan family from having their own animals grazing on their farm, but having vacant land also set the stage for their first encounter with Joe Ranger. It happened when the Coogan girls and one of their friends visiting from down country were coming up the road from a walk. When they got to the field they saw an old man with a horse taking down the gate to their fence. With self-assurance, and indignant at what was happening, the girls marched right up to him and asked what he was doing. The answer stunned them and became a cherished family story from those years.

The man was Joe Ranger. He explained that the horse was his friend and didn't have enough to eat at his house. Joe told them that every summer he and the horse would go for a walk looking for a place for the horse to stay where there was plenty of grass. He said that when they came to a field she liked, the horse would tell Joe that was where she wanted to spend the summer. This year it happened to be your field, Joe explained. As he took down the rest of the gate and let the horse in he told the girls not to worry, he would see that the gate was put back properly. Then he left. The girls instantly tore up the road to the house and breathlessly told their parents what they had seen. "You're kidding!" their parents responded. They went down to see for themselves and sure enough, there was a horse in their field. "The horse stayed there all summer," one of the daughters recounted years later, and before winter, Joe came back and got her.[9]

No doubt, the Coogans recounted the horse story to friends back

in Newton. This was the kind of Vermont experience that epitomized the native-newcomer encounter in books about the state. As
such, it was part of the attraction in coming up to visit Vermont.

Indeed, some of Peter and Barbara Coogan's friends did meet
Joe. One of their favorite walks with visitors was going up past where
Otis Wheeler lived at the Cabot place, past the old orchard at the
Howards' Udall place, and to the end of the road where it intersect-
ed with the road to the Coogans' place. In other words, the road past
Joe's.

Their circuit included not only old farms, hills, valleys, fields, and
woods, it also included Joe. Whether or not their guests thought it
wonderful, the Coogans sure did. "Everytime" they had a visitor they
wanted to impress, they "would take them on a walk and go by Joe's."
It is easy to imagine the troop making their way up and over Bunker
Hill and then descending to the Parker place where they took the road
past Joe's house. Once on the road to Joe's, the stories about him
would begin: Stories the neighbors told about Joe, stories Barbara
Coogan picked up while shopping at Finley's store in West Hartford,
and of course, the story of the horse. When Joe's place came into
sight, everyone would stare as they walked by while one of the family pointed out details about the place they had spoken of. After passing Joe's the focus of the stories changed to the Howard family as
their Udall barn complex came into sight. At the end of the day, the
visitors had been exercised and entertained. The stories about Joe
Ranger fit nicely into the Vermont "experience" the Coogans sought
to provide for their guests.[10]

One day, an encounter with Joe gave the Coogans new insight.
Whenever they had walked by Joe's with their friends it was easy to
buttress the lore that Joe preferred solace. Joe never came out of the
house. The Coogans thought this was because he didn't want visitors.
The fact was, however, that Joe was out on the road himself when

they walked by. Thus they never had encountered him at his house. That is, until the day he happened to be home.

The day the Coogans walked by Joe's and he came out of his house to greet them was doubly special. First of all, it destroyed the myth that Joe didn't like visitors. The family had thought of Joe "as someone who avoided human contact." This couldn't be further from the truth, they learned. Joe talked with them and invited them in.[11]

At the same time, however, this encounter with Joe confirmed everything else the Coogans had heard about him. He was dirty, wearing layers of clothing each in varying degrees of deterioration, and had a scruffy beard. Once inside they found a path to Joe's lair with the rest of the place "chocked full" of newspapers, boxes, and junk piled up "close to the ceiling," so tight that a "professional packer couldn't have done better." After the inside tour was finished, Joe took them out to see his berries and fruit trees. Probably it was the Coogans who decided it was time to leave, but Joe had to show them

Will and Jane Curtis. From Will Curtis, The Second Nature Of Things.

136

his barn first. Eventually they went on their way, with an enhanced understanding of Joe, and more stories.[12]

Like the Marshalls and Coogans, Will and Jane Curtis also found themselves in a position to formulate stories about their own encounters with Joe Ranger. After moving to the Gilbert place toward West Hartford in 1954, the Curtises sought to connect with the locals in the neighborhood on an equal basis. They had come to Vermont to farm and not knowing much about farming, they wanted to help and be helped by the local farmers while they learned.

They certainly needed help in their neighbor's eyes. While living in Massachusetts, Will and Jane had raised sheep and were noted for their wool and delicious lamb. They thought they could transfer their sheep business to Vermont and pick up where they had left off at their former home. While they did manage to relocate their sheep to the Gilbert farm, they quickly found they would have to convert to dairying. Sheep were looked down upon by many farmers in Vermont. They represented the era of decline and loss for Vermont farmers. While some held onto small flocks into the twentieth century, almost every farmer had completely converted to dairying by the time the Curtises arrived.

The Curtises managed to sell some lamb locally to Dartmouth professors, but that was about it. Nobody else wanted it. Ernest Howard summed it up for Will Curtis after Will brought the Howards some lamb as a neighborly present. Ernest told him to get that stuff away from him, he had had enough of mutton when he was young. If the Curtises were to be taken seriously as farmers in the neighborhood, they would have to get into dairying.

Not exactly farmers to begin with, Will and Jane were totally unfamiliar with dairying. This realization would have stymied most people with less dedication and no family support. However, the Curtises rose to the occasion. They wanted to farm. Eventually they came up with the perfect solution: They admitted they knew nothing and showed they were eager to learn. This worked, both for them and their neighbors.

The Curtises education about dairy farming began the day Will went up to Jim Clay's with a proposition. Will wanted to learn about farming, he explained, but didn't know what to do. He thought that the best way to learn would be to work with a farmer doing the seasonal and everyday chores associated with a dairy farm. How would it be, Will suggested, if he worked with Jim on the farm, without pay, to get the experience he wanted while also being a help to Jim.

Jim Clay jumped at Will Curtis' suggestion that he work for Jim on the farm for free. Hired help was hard to get and unreliable. The era had already passed when the job of necessity for the young and unemployed in rural Vermont was being a farmhand. With the mobility made possible by the automobile, people had more choices where they could work. Many local young men preferred to get jobs in area garages or shops rather than dealing with stinking cows. In allowing Will to work with him, Jim Clay acquired someone who wanted to be on the farm and was eager to work.

Through working with Jim Clay, consulting with the county agent, and maintaining enthusiasm, the Curtises were on their road to farming. They got their first cow from Jim. Later they bought ten heifers from Logan Dickey, who owned the Marshland farm in Quechee. Before long, they were shipping milk. They were farming.

Learning to farm and working their land provided the context in which Will and Jane got to know Joe Ranger. Like other newcomers, the Curtises heard about Joe before meeting him. When they finally saw him for the first time, he looked pretty much like they expected. He was a little man. He was "grimy." He was walking. And, he was carrying a stick over his shoulder with a bag on the end. They assumed he was making his way to Finley's store, but evidently, they did not speak with him.

It didn't take long, however, before Joe stopped and introduced himself to the Curtises. They were outside working and when Joe spied them, he made a beeline to them. No doubt, meeting and speaking with him fulfilled their expectations. He had stories. Among the stories remembered by Jane were the ones dealing with health. By the sound of it, Joe had a cure for almost anything. He told them he "drank porcupine blood mixed with kerosene." It wasn't clear exactly what he was curing with that mixture, but the most important thing he claimed that kept him healthy was that he didn't have to eat "no danged woman's cookin."[13]

The Curtises were charmed by Joe. When they got a chance they hiked up to see him in his own domain. Joe showed them his beaver pond and invited them into his house. They saw his stove, table, chair, and bed crammed into one corner of the house. He showed them the place in the wall where the honeybees had established a colony. When he wanted some honey, he told them, he "just reached in through a hole in the wall and fetched out a fistful." His firewood and potatoes were right at hand, piled inside the house among his furnishings. All he needed to buy, he claimed, "was some coffee and tinned meat."[14]

Like others, Will and Jane Curtis dubbed Joe a "character," but at the time they did not feel he should be put on show for others. They never brought any of their friends up to see him. That would have been "rather imposing" on Joe, they felt. Despite all the interaction they had with Joe, they still thought he only "liked company in moderation."[15]

While the Curtises did not openly celebrate and promote Joe out of respect for his privacy, a larger reason for their silence was hinted at years later. Sitting in his home in Woodstock village, Will Curtis recalled that time when he and Jane "lived the farming life." Those years had gone by fast because they were very busy. Their biggest concern was getting their farm going and succeeding. And when you come down to it, they only lived on the Gilbert place a few years. They had quickly realized it was too small to be profitable. To continue farming, they had to get a bigger farm and so they sold the old Gilbert place and bought another one in Hartland.[16]

Even though Will and Jane Curtis did not "have the time" during their years on the Quechee-West Hartford road to imagine Joe Ranger as anything bigger than he was to them at the time, they later realized the possibilities of Joe's story. He represented a bygone era. He was self-sufficient. He lived his life simply. The Curtises just didn't have the time when they lived near Joe to "sit down and write about him." They "should have taken the time," Will reflected, it would have been easier and more accurate back then to record the facts about Joe and his world.[17] As it turned out, accuracy was one of the things that got lost with time when the Curtises finally did write about Joe, years later. However, by that point it didn't matter. The memory of Joe Ranger was integrated into bigger concerns which we will explore in chapter 12.

9

Fame

Joe Ranger's expanded notoriety during the 1950s and 1960s resulted in his becoming one of the most photographed faces in Vermont. Interest in Joe coincided with an expansion of interest in photography and both amateur and professional photographers got out their cameras and sought appropriate subjects. In Joe, they found the perfect character. Visually, he had all the hallmarks of what many photographers were seeking. He was old, he had a scraggly beard, his clothes were mismatched, patched, and dirty. He was also incredibly quotable. Equally important, Joe was a willing participant.

Burton Wheeler claimed that Joe loved to be photographed. Burt knew firsthand, because he himself photographed Joe. He remembered Joe as more than willing to have his picture taken and that he would even submit to being directed and staged. On one occasion Burt was using his movie camera to film Joe. Burt had him walk to a spot, stop, and as the film neared the end, Burt told Joe to take off his hat and take a bow. Joe obliged.[1]

The first striking aspect of the surviving photographs of Joe Ranger is that they were all taken when he was old. This is under-

Joe Ranger at the entrance to his barn. Photo: Damon Jillson

standable. More people were taking casual pictures in the postwar ere, but more importantly, before World War II no one had any reason to photograph Joe. At that time he was only a poor, dirty, witty, man. The conditions were not right for Joe to be considered special. It wasn't until after the war that people, egged on by the growing fascination with Vermont characters, took out their cameras to photograph them. By the time people started to take special notice of characters like Joe, he was already over seventy years old.[2]

Along with Joe being old, the photographs all show him in his natural setting, including some inside his house. These of course, show the squalor Joe lived in.

There is a photograph of Joe in his barn. He is milking his cow. This picture naturally sets Joe in the realm of farmer. However, because the picture is of him and his only cow, it also shows that farming had declined significantly from the days when there would have been other cows in the barn. There is also a photo of Joe standing in the doorway of the barn. If there was any doubt that Joe Ranger's farming days were all but over, one only need see the condition of the barn in this image.

Most photographs of Joe, however, were taken outside. Some were taken with Joe standing in front of his house. There are a couple of "action shots" showing Joe with an armful of firewood and drinking from a jug. One photo shows Joe standing by the beaver pond where he spent so much time. And there are photographs that focus entirely on Joe without any recognizable location in the background.

Many of the photographs of Joe in this sample were taken by his neighbors. Naturally, as Joe's popularity rose, those living nearest him also wanted pictures of him. The campaign to attract newcomers to rural Vermont had not only succeeded in weaving an image aimed at outsiders. Natives also accepted the idea of Vermont and Vermont characters as special. This phenomenon is buttressed by the fact that the photos taken of Joe by his neighbors do not predate those taken by others from outside the region. They all date from 1955-1964.[3]

Neighbors who took Joe's pictures included Burton Wheeler, Damon Jillson, and Leslie Hazen. Burton Wheeler had grown up in the neighborhood and after living in Wilder, Vermont, during his youth, he came back and bought a house, just down the hill from the Cabot place where his brother Otis was caretaker. Damon Jillson had grown up in Pomfret and later moved to Somerville, Massachusetts, but he never lost the ties to his hometown and came back often. Leslie Hazen was a native of Hartford and had known Joe as a kid.[4] Burton Wheeler took many different pictures of Joe. There are photographs of times the Wheelers and their nephew, Norman Picken, went up to Joe's to "celebrate" Norman and Joe's birthdays, which were only a few days apart. There were photographs of Joe by himself, and home movies of Joe.

The photograph Damon Jillson took of Joe shows him standing in the doorway to his barn. The image is blurry, but it clearly shows Joe smiling with his old clothes and deteriorating barn.[5]

Leslie Hazen took still photographs of Joe. But he also dreamed about making a movie about him. In that effort he used countless reels of home movie film. Although a movie never resulted, Hazen kept the collection and loved to talk about it in his old age.[6]

Neighbors were not the only ones who were interested in taking Joe's picture. Wayne Thompson used Joe as part of a college photography project before beginning a career in photography and art. Thompson grew up in Woodstock and his father was a native of South Pomfret. The elder Thompson knew Joe since his own youth and in later years, when hunting in Joe's neighborhood, he would stop in occasionally. Wayne Thompson had only seen Joe once or twice since he was a kid and really didn't attach any importance to him.[7]

During a college photography class in the early 1960s Thompson was charged with a project to photograph people in their everyday endeavors. The idea was to get the images of ordinary people. His focus was to be the folks around his own hometown.

Years later, Wayne Thompson could not remember if it was his father or himself who first thought of including Joe Ranger in this project. The elder Thompson had learned over the years to appreciate Joe as a local character and he may have suggested that Wayne go see him. Either way, father and son both became interested in local characters.

Among the characters visited by the Thompsons were George and Alice Chamberlin, brother and sister, who lived on an old farm on the side of the Delectable Mountains in neighboring Barnard. Single, old fashioned, and isolated, the Chamberlins were the epitome of their "type" portrayed in books highlighting Vermont's land and people. Although intensely shy, the Chamberlins welcomed the Thompsons and enjoyed visiting with them.

Another character interesting to the Thompsons was "Perley" Wheeler. Whereas the Chamberlins preferred limiting their exposure to the outside world, Wheeler thrived on it. He lived on the back side of the Suicide Six ski area in South Pomfret and through his employment at the ski area he became *the* Vermont character there. He didn't own a car and would snowshoe over the hill to the ski area to work. Dressed in his plaid wool jacket and hat, Perley collected the lift tickets from skiers and dispensed witticisms to the delight of the public as well as his managers. He was the "local color" at Suicide Six and was also photographed by Wayne Thompson.

Thus, including local characters such as Joe Ranger in his college photography project in 1962 came naturally to Wayne Thompson. Although his 1962 compilation no longer exists intact, his photograph of Joe Ranger does.[8]

Joe Ranger by Collamer Abbott

The photographs that Burt Wheeler and Damon Jillson took of Joe Ranger were seen only by friends and neighbors. Those taken by Leslie Hazen and Wayne Thompson, although taken with a wider audience in mind, also had limited exposure. In contrast the photographs taken by journalists were seen by many. Collamer Abbott and Hanson Carroll took photos of Joe in the 1950s for the regional newspaper, the *Valley News*. Although only one of these photographers was successful in getting his images printed during Joe's lifetime, the story of how these two men approached Joe Ranger and imagined the story their photographs would tell, puts into perspective the evolution of how Joe's image was perceived and promoted.

There were important differences in Collamer Abbott and Hanson Carroll's backgrounds, which influenced their approaches toward photographing Joe. Collamer Abbott was a native of the area with limited means while Hanson Carroll was from out of the area and financially secure.

Abbott was raised in Wilder, Vermont, and developed an interest in newspaper work while in high school when he and several of his classmates started a school paper, "The Smudge." The experience set the course for Abbott's future. He wanted to be a writer. Throughout his life he wrote for various papers, journals, and publications.[9]

Abbott started out his career with the *Brattleboro Reformer*. The *Reformer* was a daily dedicated to state and local news. There Collamer Abbott imbibed the doctrine that a reporter should get all the facts and report those facts in a balanced way. This no-nonsense approach suited Abbott well. He organized his life so fairness in his reporting was uninfluenced by personal relationships. Abbott purposefully avoided making close friends in the community because news could happen to anyone. He feared that if he ever found himself reporting about a friend, he might slant the story in their favor, or lose their friendship.

Abbott's journalistic principles, and the desire to write, stuck with him. After leaving the *Reformer* he worked at the *Bennington Banner* as the editorial page editor for several months until he realized the pace was killing him. Wanting to continue writing, Abbott and his wife took a huge gamble and went to France in 1952 with no money and a desire to see the people he had met during the war, and write. During their three-month trip the Abbotts stayed with several of Collamer's friends and poked around the country, exploring whatever caught their fancy. The result of this trip was a cementing of former friendships and the production of eleven articles that Abbott was able to sell. Later in life he claimed that he was never able to reproduce the success he had with these French pieces.

After the trip to France, Abbott needed a job. He found one at the *Valley News*, the recently established daily newspaper based in Lebanon, New Hampshire. In 1952 the *Valley News* replaced *The Landmark*, an old weekly White River Junction paper dedicated to advertising and community gossip.[10]

While *The Landmark* was an old-style local paper established in the nineteenth century, the *Valley New* was established by a group of more modern journalists. Their goal was not only to report the news, but to battle within their newspaper's pages what they perceived to be wrong in the Upper Valley. That style of reporting and writing was prominent in their paper.

This agenda-driven style of the *Valley News* was different than what Collamer Abbott was used to. Years later, he remembered the editors telling him "how to report" stories to conform to their agenda. They would pick what they thought was important, "play it up," and inject their own liberal ideas of what the story was about. One of the reports about a Norwich town meeting that Abbott wrote in the "old style" of reporting was rejected and changed. He had covered the meeting with the intention of capturing "the gist of the whole" – to provide an overview of the whole meeting. Abbott's editors, however, were more interested in focusing on one or two contentious aspects of the meeting rather than summarizing the whole.[11] These differences in perspective and style between the editors and Abbott initially were not a major problem. Collamer Abbott wasn't hired as a reporter. Although he did occasionally report news and write articles for the *Valley News*, he was originally hired as a photographer. Abbott had previous experience with cameras and film, so he was chosen to be the main photographer for the paper. Most of his writing for the paper was for the captions to his photographs.

Abbott spent most of his days with his camera. He was either out on the road looking for interesting images to capture, attending meetings and events, or rushing to accident scenes. In the four years he worked for the *Valley News* in the mid-1950s, Collamer Abbott literally took thousands of photographs of life in the Upper Valley. His collection of photographs remains a monument to his work and a document of a place in time.

It was while working for the *Valley News* that Collamer Abbott met, and photographed, Joe Ranger. One day at the paper, Mike DeSherbinin went into the darkroom to see Abbott. "There's a guy out in Pomfret who talks to beaver," he said "Go get him." DeSherbinin and the other editors at the *Valley News* were primed and ready to pick up on things having to do with "old Vermonters" like Joe Ranger. DeSherbinin had heard about Joe and thought a photo and caption, or a full story, about this old native talking to animals would make a nice human interest piece. It would show some of the "local color" of the region.

Abbott thought the idea of an old guy talking to beaver was crazy, but he went looking for Joe. He made his way to West Hartford and to the road where, he was told, Joe lived. After "gingerly" driving up the grade and down past the old Udall barn, Abbott went over the next grade and saw two beaver ponds off to the right. Thinking he was near, he came upon "something that resembled a house" and figured this was the Ranger place.[12]

Abbott stepped out of his car, Abbott walked toward the door, and hollered if anybody was home. A loud greeting came from inside and out came Joe. Years later, Collamer Abbott remembered what Joe Ranger looked like, but didn't remember their conversation. "I told him what I was looking for" and "he led me across the road and down a path to [the] pond." Joe began calling, "Billy, Billy. Cum Billy. Cum Billy." Meanwhile, Abbott tried "to suppress [his] skepticism and be patient." There was a stick-and-mud beaver house out in the pond, but "Everything was quiet and tranquil." Joe continued calling. "This went on for quite some time" and in the end Abbott's "skepticism was confirmed." No beaver talk. "We wound our way back to the road," he remembered. Abbott then snapped Joe's picture "and parted with Joe Ranger for the first and last time." There was no story here. No doubt, Mike DeSherbinin was disappointed.

The failure of Collamer Abbott to get a story about Joe Ranger for the *Valley News* highlights an important difference between him and his editors. Abbott was a no-nonsense reporter. He didn't go for fantasy making. Joe Ranger was just an old guy "living his own life." "What difference [did] it make?" Collamer Abbott saw nothing special about Joe.[13]

But while Collamer Abbott didn't see Joe Ranger as any sort of "typical" or "unique" Vermonter, the guys back at the *Valley News* did. They "had a totally different idea of what was going on up here." They were from places like Brooklyn, graduated from colleges like Dartmouth, married educated, well-connected women, socialized with their peers, and played along with the growing popular notion that Vermont and Vermonters were special. They simply went nuts over natives like Joe. "Any Vermonter who was the least bit a

Vermonter" as to actions, accent, and outlook, Abbott claimed, were celebrated by these guys. "You know," Abbott recalled, "they'd [even] make jokes of me and my accent for crying out loud." One time Abbott came into the office after driving in a nasty snowstorm. DeSherbinin asked him how the driving was and Abbott simply replied that "it's ok if you stay in the road." DeSherbinin nearly tipped over in his chair. "He laughed like hell because" to his ear "this was a typical local response" a Vermonter would give. Abbott felt he was looked on as the paper's local native who could be entertaining while being useful.[14]

Even though Collamer Abbott hadn't bought into the idea that Vermonters like Joe Ranger should be celebrated, another photographer who had recently started working for the paper, did. Hanson Carroll recognized Joe as a character worthy of being photographed and produced photos of him, which in 1957 were seen by almost everybody in the Upper Valley. Carroll had the skill, connections, and correct viewpoint to succeed in promoting his photographs of Joe, even on a national scale.

Carroll made his living from photography. His forte was the Vermont landscape peopled by Vermonters. During this era of interest in Vermont rural images, Carroll spent his days traveling the State looking for images he thought would sell. Farmers working in the field with a background including hills or a valley were marketable. If the farmer was using horses, all the better. Sometimes he was able to make a good photograph better by including children in it. Many times he used his own kids. One example he recalled was coming upon a pasture with a horse grazing. It was ok. However, it would be better if there was a girl riding that horse. Carroll got a little girl to climb onto the horse and the subsequent photograph provided a perfect image of rural innocence.

Carroll's prime market for his photographs was *Vermont Life*. Over the years he worked closely with the magazine's editors to provide the images that promoted the rural idyll the state's leaders wanted to portray. In this, Carroll was considered the master. Indeed, the ultimate measure of his success with *Vermont Life* was the fact that he contributed the most cover photographs, a record he still holds to this day.

Even though Hanson Carroll's name later became synonymous with *Vermont Life,* in the mid-1950s he was still trying to make a name for himself. Carroll's first wife had money so he didn't have to put most of his effort into making a living at that point in his life. He instead worked at developing his craft, periodically working on other projects part time. One of these was doing photography work for the *Valley News.* Doing part-time work for the newspaper fit right in with his goals. The editorial staff liked Carroll and they came up with an agreement to accommodate his independent work. He could do the

Joe Ranger by Hanson Carroll.

152

newspaper work and his own at the same time. If he was on the trail of a picture for the paper and he came across an image of a scene he could use for himself, he could capture it and then go back to what he was doing for the paper. It was a charmed arrangement.

During this period of photographing for the *Valley News*, Hanson Carroll encountered Joe Ranger, though years later, he could not recall meeting or photographing Joe. After thousands of photographs and a house fire in 1989, which destroyed his notes, photographs, and negative collection, Carroll tries not to look back. Perhaps someone at *the Valley News* tipped him off about Joe. Mike DeSherbinin certainly had heard about him.[15]

It is also possible that Carroll stumbled upon Joe Ranger while out looking for scenes to photograph. He made sure to travel the back roads of Pomfret every foliage season because it was one of his favorite places. Carroll once said that he thought Pomfret and Peacham, Vermont, were among the best places to photograph. Both contained all the elements of what the editors of *Vermont Life* wanted: scenic rolling hills, farms, a white church with a steeple. Although Pomfret's people were not sought after, Carroll did include folks at the Harrington place and the Moore farm in two of his subsequent *Vermont Life* covers.[16]

While Joe Ranger was not cover material for *Vermont Life*, Hanson Carroll registered him in his mind as a photogenic character who might come in handy some day. That time came sooner, rather than later. Carroll learned that Joe was well known locally and widely photographed. It didn't take long for Carroll to come up with an idea. Since quite a number of people in the region had heard of Joe Ranger but had never met him, and since there were legions of other folks who didn't know he existed, Carroll would introduce Joe to the Upper Valley. The plan was to photograph and interview Joe for the *Valley News*.

Hanson Carroll set out to photograph Joe just after New Years' Day, 1957. The snow was deep that January and Carroll drove as far as the road to Joe's allowed. Upon his arrival, Joe welcomed Carroll and invited him into the house. He must have spent all morning with Joe. They talked and Joe showed Carroll his house, barn, books, and animals. Carroll snapped pictures left and right. Notes were taken and by the time he left, Hanson Carroll had decided what was noteworthy about Joe.

On January 7, 1957, the Upper Valley was introduced to Joe Ranger. He was on the front page of the *Valley News*. The photograph featured Joe outside with an armful of firewood and his house in the background. He was bareheaded and his face was dirty. The yard was snowbound, the woodpile amply covered with several inches. The house was unpainted. Just by looking at the picture it was easy to see that he was not your average Joe.

To make sure everyone understood that Joe was special the caption under the photograph in bold letters introduced him as "ONE OF THIS AREA'S MOST COLORFUL CHARACTERS." Referring to Joe as an "81-year-old hermit" who "leads a life of complete solitude," the paper stated that he "spends his Winters reading westerns and detective stories" and is "interrupted only occasionally to go outside and get a few sticks of wood for his fire." Joe lived in a "one-room house" and "sees people about once a month when he walks five miles to West Hartford for a minimum of supplies." Ending up with a quote from this "native Vermonter" about never being married, everyone who looked at the paper that evening was told that here was a Vermont original. And there was more.[17]

The bottom line of text crediting Carroll as the photographer informed readers that there were other photos of Ranger on page 5. Opening to that page, readers found three more pictures with text. The first showed Joe fondling a head of cabbage with a quote about

154

it being his last one for the winter. Not only did he lack cabbage, "the hermit" lived "two miles from any accessible road." But that was all right, because if the snow got heavy and he couldn't get out to get supplies he could "always make pancakes with a sack of flour" he had in his house. "In spite of the hardships Ranger is a happy man who welcomes visitors but prefers not to leave his backwoods home except about once a month to get more stores."[18]

The next photo showed Joe looking over one of his books. "ANOTHER DAY, ANOTHER BOOK TO READ." Along with showing Joe's interest in books, the picture also gave a hint of the mess that was his house. In the background is a huge pile of papers and trash upon which two of his cats are comfortably seated. The last photograph features Joe kneeling by the side of his cow. Besides reading and "chopping wood for his stove," Joe also milks his cow "twice a day." Finally, Carroll soberly informed his readers that Joe "has supported himself since he was 12."[19]

It is hard to gauge the effect Hanson Carroll's photo's of Joe had on Upper Valley residents. The *Valley News* had a wide circulation in the region and most people picking up the newspaper naturally looked at the front page first. On January 7th readers found an old man, a "character," a "hermit," smiling back at them. After reading the captions accompanying the pictures, it is doubtful many raced out to look up Joe. However, it planted a seed in people's minds. In their midst lived a hermit with a memorable name.[20]

The one place we can see an increased interest in Joe Ranger during the late 1950s is in his own diary. Previously, Joe wrote down most of his interactions with his neighbors and none with the people he didn't know. Since Joe didn't have any idea who many of those who dropped by were, he didn't write about them. However, after his photograph appeared in the *Valley News*, entries about these nameless visitors appear. During the 1957 fall foliage season people flocked to

Joe's. On October 5th he noted, "had my Picture taken." How many times he didn't say. He also only hinted at newcomers when he described them as "friends." On the 12th he "gave some apples" to some of these new friends, whom he also described as "company." One group he elaborated on because they were special: "had [my] picture taken with 4 girls," he wrote in October 1958. During the summer and fall of 1959 he had "16 folks here" on July 19th, eighteen on the 21st, and on August 2nd he "had folks here all the forenoon." Once foliage season rolled around again, more people came. On September 26th Joe noted that he had a phenomenal "30 folks" at his place that day. Joe's diary only gives us a glimpse of the increased interest he received. Come 1962 there would be even more.[21]

In 1962 Hanson Carroll did it again. The Hermit's photograph made another appearance. This time Carroll succeeded in publishing Joe's photo in one of the nation's most popular regional magazines, with a wider circulation than *Vermont Life*: *Yankee*.

Yankee readers across the country opened their January 1962 issue and found Joe Ranger staring out at them from page 29. The photograph shows Joe sitting in his chair holding one of his cats. His Glenwood stove sits prominently in the foreground, reassuring readers that Joe stayed warm. And it is easy to see that Joe Ranger was no housekeeper. In fact this last aspect of the photograph was the theme of the story. Joe's photograph was one of a pair on a two-page spread entitled, "Order and Disorder." Opposite Joe's picture was one of an immaculate china cabinet arranged very "orderly." Everything was in its right place. Joe, on the other hand, was represented as the master of disorder.[22]

The caption for the spread had nothing to do with the china cabinet and everything to do with Joe. In language echoing the earlier *Valley News* piece, it described Joe as a "bachelor-hermit" who lived "two miles from any accessible road." Starting his day "at 4:30 A.M.," he "milks his cow, chops his wood and reads books" before retiring "at 8:00 P.M." Although simple, Joe was resourceful. If the weather was bad and he couldn't go out to get groceries, he "could always make pancakes" with the stores he regularly kept on hand.[23]

The publication of Joe Ranger's photograph in *Yankee* came about during Hanson Carroll's search for Vermont images. His realization that a local "character" would be of interest to those living outside of Joe's neighborhood reflected the increased focus on rural native New Englanders since the Depression, as exemplified by the parade of books, articles, columns, and photographs, that were subsequently published. Perhaps Carroll was simply following the trend. He provided the public with the images of Vermont they wanted.

It may be true that photographers like Carroll were following a trend. The mania for Vermont and Vermonters after the 1930s had many followers. However, at the same time they were following, they were also creating. The combined efforts of individual "followers" made the Vermont image. State officials, authors, natives, newcomers, and photographers all had a hand in the process. State officials conceived of and guided the image. Writers promoted it. Natives learned to play along with it. Newcomers bought into it. And photographers documented it. Hanson Carroll is best known as one of the premier creators of classic Vermont photographs. Less known is that he also helped transform a poor, dirty, little old man into a Vermont character.

10

Exit

Joe Ranger may have achieved fame, but he continued to struggle during his last years. One of his struggles again involved the town of Pomfret. Town officials sought to oust Joe from his home in order to "help" him, and, coincidentally, save the town money in the process. Joe was the only person living on his stretch of road and the selectmen wanted him to move to North Pomfret Village during the winter months so the town wouldn't have to spend the time, effort, and money keeping his place plowed out. Joe resisted initially, but finally consented.

During the winters of 1959-60 and 1960-61, Joe lived in North Pomfret in a house recently vacated by a woman who was a town charge. His days there were spent much the same as when he was at his own house. However, after two winters of living away from home, Joe Ranger stayed put and luckily for him, the town resumed plowing him out.

Snow plowing in the 1950s was different than it is today. Whereas today, plows go out during the storm to keep the roads clear, back then, the emphasis was only on keeping the main roads clear while the smaller side roads were left untouched until the storm ended. Once the storm was over, the town plow trucks would make the rounds cleaning out the side roads. The first side roads to get cleared were the ones traveled by milk trucks. Milk trucks had to get to the farms to pick up the farmers milk daily: farmer's livelihoods depended on it. Since Pomfret still supported numerous farms in the 1950s, the roads to these farms were the first priority to clear during winter.

The second round of plowing out the side roads targeted areas where a number of families resided. If milk trucks had to get to the farms, Pomfret's commuting workers had to get to their work. For many leaving town for work, the route was all downhill. Navigating through snow could be impossible when climbing a hill, but was easier when the trip was down a steady grade. Most of Pomfret's commuters had to deal with unplowed roads at least a few days of the winter when they went to work in the morning, but the roads were cleaned out by the time they came back home from work.

The Cabot place and road leading to Joe Ranger's. Photo: Collamer Abbott

The last roads to get plowed out were the ones where only one house was located. Several residences in Pomfret were at the end of dead-end roads. Some were occupied year-round, but a couple were only used seasonally. It was easy to delegate these as the last to get cleared out.[1]

Joe Ranger's house was not at the end of a dead-end road, but it might as well have been. While kept up in the summer with no problem, the town had given up trying to keep the whole stretch open in the winter. The problem was the part between Joe's and Albert Parker's old place. Once leaving Joe's, the road climbs a steep grade that is narrow and tree lined until the crest of the hill at Parker's. The plows had an awful time getting through here. There was no room to pass an oncoming car. There was no place to put the snow. In short, it was a pain-in-the-ass.[2]

Eventually, town officials decided that they did not need to plow the whole road. Only part would be kept open in winter. The plan was to keep open the section open from Alice Wood's place in Hartford up to Joe Ranger's, thus giving access to all who needed to travel the road, including Wood, the Marshalls, the Howards, and Joe. The only hitch to this plan was that the Pomfret plow trucks would have to drive from Pomfret down to West Hartford and up the Quechee Road to Wood's house and then to the Pomfret line before plowing. This was a major drive for such a short stretch of road. Negotiations were conducted and and agreement finalized with the town of Hartford so that whichever town's plow trucks got to Alice Wood's first, that truck would clean out the whole stretch from Wood's to Joe Ranger's place.[3]

Even with accommodating agreements to share/trade plowing, the Town of Pomfret spent a lot of money on its winter roadwork. Winter maintenance represented around 25% of the town's total highway expenses in the 1950s. And the cost of maintaining the town's roads was climbing higher every year. The town budget for highway expenses went from over $36,000 in 1954 to over $40,000 by 1957.[4]

Higher costs of keeping up and open the town's highways in the later 1950s combined with a squeeze on revenue, Pomfret's selectmen reported. In 1959, the receipts "in the Highway Accounts of $16,848.03 from the State Treasurer was $10,512.97 less than the Budget estimate of $27,361.00." Pomfret was getting less money than they anticipated from the state. The 1960 town report informed residents that "Attention" should be paid "to the fact that for the past two years Expenses of [the] Town have exceeded Receipts." In 1959 the imbalance was $1,444.73 and in 1960, $1,170.41.[5]

One response to less revenue was to squeeze money out elsewhere. In their 1957 report, the selectmen proudly informed Pomfret's citizens that those who were behind in their taxes were being squeezed. "Delinquent Tax Collections in 1957 were unusually large. Without these collections there would have been a substantial loss" to the town. "The Constable, Ric Davis, is to be congratulated for his contribution" in harassing the delinquent and accomplishing "this favorable result."[6]

Trying to get by without raising the town's tax rate, Pomfret's officials sought places where they could cut spending. Winter snow plowing was an obvious place to focus. In particular, those stretches of road deemed unnecessary to keep open to winter traffic were scrutinized. Roads with summer homes at the end were considered for receiving less winter maintenance, as was the road from the Alice Wood place to the Albert Parker place, which Joe Ranger lived on. The only problem with not plowing this road was what to do about Joe.

Scott Harrington was working for the Pomfret highway department during this time and remembers the town's attempt to move Joe out of his house so his road could be left unplowed. Moses Chase was Pomfret's road commissioner at the time and Harrington's boss. The selectmen got together with Chase to discuss their ideas for where Joe could spend winters. Someone suggested that an unused chicken coop on the old Dr. Bugbee place could work. Figuring that Joe wasn't much of a housekeeper, he wouldn't mind living where hens had been. Evidently, this proposal was taken seriously and one of the selectmen went to see if Joe would go along with the idea. Scott Harrington didn't hear what Joe told the selectman, but Moses Chase did. Chase summed up by telling Harrington that he guessed Joe wouldn't be going over there.[7]

The next attempt at getting Joe to leave his home for winter succeeded. The selectmen proposed that Joe move into the old Burch house, down across the road from the church. The Burch place had recently become vacant when Catherine Burch could no longer live there on her own. Burch was the widow of Ed Burch, who always said he was writing a book, and barely worked enough to support his large family. Various neighbors had later helped provide employment for the kids in the family, but Catherine Burch later became a town charge. As a result of her care by the town and inability to pay her property taxes, the town took over her house. Thus, being empty, and in the town's care, it became the logical place for Joe Ranger to spend his winters.[8]

We don't know how the approach to Joe was made this time, or how long it took to convince him. However, the town eventually prevailed. On the first of December, 1959, Joe wrote that he had "got things to gether to go over to North Pomfret." Two days later he "went over to the Birch house to live this winter." Joe was in North Pomfret Village and the town could forgo plowing out his place.[9]

Joe's winter at the Burch house was pretty much just like any other. He read and kept up the fire in the stove. Ever since he stopped having cattle to care for, Joe spent much of the winter and inclement weather reading. Between January and May, 1958, Joe "red and got in wood" 104 days. When the weather got warm in May, he tended to his berries and garden until fall, when at the end of October he began reading again, and tending the stove. Fifty-seven additional days were spent with book in hand the last part of 1958, including every day in December.[10]

Joe kept up this same winter routine for as long as he lived at the Burch house. It is easy to see why. With a lot of time and no chores, reading entertained him and passed the days. Some of his books survive, four of them by Max Brand, the writer of western novels. We can only guess that Joe brought at least some of his books with him to the Burch house in December 1959 when he mentioned getting his "things to gether" to go.[11]

Although Joe spent much of his time reading and tending to his fire, he was not completely housebound in North Pomfret. He got out. He walked over to Earle Harrington's old store, now operated by his son, Stuart Harrington, for groceries or chewing tobacco. Sometimes he went down to West Hartford to Ruby Smith's store, as he did after first arriving at the Burch house. Smith's store was larger than Harrington's and Joe spent $15 there as opposed to the 20 cents or 49 cents he spent at Stuart's.[12]

Joe still visited folks while living at the Burch house and in fact was closer to his Pomfret friends. On January 28, 1959 he "went to harry harringtons to dinner" and another day Harry's sister-in-law Gail stopped by to see Joe. Someone in the village also drove him to White River Junction whenever Joe needed to go there.

Although the winter went by, come March, Joe was thinking about home again. He had walked back over only once to check on his place after first coming to North Pomfret, but he had not been back since. Planning ahead, Joe "payd out 9.00 for trees and Berry

Bushes" on March 8th so they would arrive and be ready to set out at his place after he got back home. On April 12 he simply wrote, "Moved home to day."[13]

That first winter Joe Ranger spent at the Burch place passed fairly uneventfully. Although the winter of 1959-1960 passed without any major upsets, it appears the next season Joe spent in North Pomfret was anything but tranquil.

Because no diary of Joe's survives documenting the winter of 1960-1961, all the information we have comes from the diaries of Albert Parker and Otis Wheeler. Parker had moved from his old farm into the house next to the North Pomfret church back in 1949 and was later a selectman and overseer of the poor, so his entries deal with Joe from the perspective of a town official having responsibility for Joe. It was Parker who went over to Joe's to talk to him about getting ready for the move to the Burch house. On October 16th Parker went over to see Joe as he had the previous October. He probably expected some sort of protest or resistance, but got none. This time, Joe simply had a list of things he wanted done at the Burch house before he would move in.[14]

Wanting to accommodate Joe, and get him to the Burch place well before snow fell, Albert spent the 25th tinkering "at [the] Burch place for Joe." Although we don't know what Albert worked on that day, he spent another day in November setting up Joe's stove. On the day Joe moved back in, Albert had gone down early and "built up [the] fires for Joe" so the house would be warm when he arrived.[15]

Albert probably thought that Joe was now all set for the winter. Joe could work on getting in the wood from the pile the town got up for him outside the door, and spend the rest of the time reading and visiting the store and neighbors. If Albert thought Joe's, and his own, winter would be trouble-free, he was wrong. He would be kept busy doing things for Joe until Joe went back home the following April.

After getting Joe settled in, Albert went on December 10th to see how he was getting along. Joe was certainly getting along fine. However, before Albert left, Joe complained about the door. So, a few days later, Albert "put [a door] latch on for Joe." Before Albert got away this time, Joe complained about the condition of a chair. On the 30th Albert "repaired [the] chair for Joe." Once the New Year came, Joe had no new projects for Albert. But he had other errands he wanted Albert to do for him. Joe asked Albert to take him "down to Stetsons."[16]

Lloyd Stetson was a handyman and talker, and Joe seems to have enjoyed having Albert take him to Stetson's for conversation and to get his saw filed. No doubt, the visits were long. After the initial visit, Joe had Albert drive him down a couple times more. Perhaps Albert got sick of waiting around while Lloyd Stetson jabbered on, for the next time Joe asked Albert about going to Stetson's to get his saw filed, Albert took it down himself and left Joe behind.[17]

Four days after pulling this trick on Joe, however, Albert got his coming up. Joe's water froze. Apparently an act of nature, it is easy to imagine that the water at the Burch place needed to be left dripping in the sink so as not to freeze in the winter. However, it is also easy to imagine Joe turning off the water completely, allowing the water to freeze and forcing Albert to provide him with water. For the next several weeks Albert "took water down to Joe" until he finally "Thawed out Joes water" on April 15th. Luckily for Albert, Joe went home shortly afterward instead of coming up with another project for him to do.[18]

It would appear that Albert had enough of Joe that winter. Once Joe went back home, Albert never went over to see him until mid-August. He only went again in October to talk about the coming winter, and Joe's move. Fortunately for Parker, and happily for Joe, Joe told Albert he was staying put at home the coming winter. Parker didn't argue and that winter the town plowed Joe out, and did so for the remainder of his life.[19]

Was Joe Ranger a big pain-in-the-ass for Albert Parker during the winter of 1960-1961? Parker's diary suggests that he was. One could assume that Parker as the overseer of the poor didn't encourage Joe to move to the Burch house the next winter because he didn't want to deal with Joe's complaints and tricks. Such an inference, however, would be inaccurate. Albert Parker was well versed in dealing with residents of every stripe throughout the many years he held town offices. This long experience, combined with a personality dedicated to duty, kept Parker from shirking his responsibility.

The real reason Joe Ranger was not forced to go back to the Burch house again was financial. The town was simply back in the black. After reporting that the town's expenses had "exceeded Receipts" in 1959 and 1960, the selectmen in their 1961 report gleefully reported that the current "estimated Receipts and Expenses results in an estimated GAIN of $9,550.00 for 1962." The selectmen suggested that as a result of this gain, "we recommend that the tax rate for the Town be reduced" so that the excess would be given back to the taxpayers. It appears, however, that the town allocated enough money to keep Joe Ranger plowed out.[20]

The town ended up keeping Joe's road open: that was a help. The biggest help Joe received in his old age, however, was from Otis Wheeler. Since the days when they used to spat with each other, the two appear to have held a truce in the late 1950s, which lasted as long as Joe lived. One can get a good idea of the transformation in their relationship from Otis Wheeler's extant diaries. In Otis' earlier diaries Joe is rarely mentioned. In 1939 Otis and Joe were probably fuming over a fight they'd had. On the second of January, Otis wrote that "Joe came down" and they "went over to Burches Mill" to pick up some lumber. More than likely, Otis hired Joe to give him a hand.

The next and only other mention of Joe that year was three days later, when Otis sourly noted that he had gone up to do some work at his parental home, expecting Joe's help, but "Joe didn't show up."[21]

The next diary we have for Otis is from 1949, and although Joe is mentioned in it more frequently, their interactions were strictly business, mainly Joe doing work for Otis. Otis "fixed fence" a few days and "Joe helped." One day at the end of June, Joe cultivated corn for Otis and then in the second week of July he worked in Otis' garden. For his part, Otis went up and "plowed garden for Joe" in May, but that was about all Otis did for Joe. This state of affairs eventually changed.[22]

By the early 1960s Otis was all but waiting on Joe hand and foot. Numerous entries in Otis' diary depict him helping Joe with odd jobs, getting his mail, picking up his groceries, and taking Joe wherever he needed to go. In 1961 Otis still noted Joe only a few times in his diary, but every one of the entries was in reference to Otis helping or checking on Joe instead of Joe working for Otis. Wheeler "went up to Joes" twice between April 20th and the first of December, but then began a routine that kept him in almost weekly contact with Joe for the next three years. Joe had always walked to the stores in West Hartford, Quechee, and North Pomfret to get groceries, but on December 19, 1961, Otis "Went to White River [Jct.] got Joes groceries [and] took them up to him."[23]

From January to December 1962, Otis Wheeler noted in his diary helping or seeing Joe a total fifty-four times. While a plethora of entries merely say he "Went up to Joes," or took "Joes groceries up to him," we also get a more complicated picture of the details involved in helping Joe. Sometimes Otis made special trips for seemingly trivial items such as a pouch of chewing tobacco when Joe was out. At times getting to Joe's was a challange as road conditions wouldn't allow Otis to drive. Since January, Otis had gone up regularly to see

Joe without writing how he had got there, but then on February 25 he noted that he "started for Joes with [the] tractor" but "didn't make it." Otis did make it the next week, when he "took groceries to Joes."[24]

Along with handling necessities, such as groceries and mail - including Joe's "money;" his cashed state check - Otis also bought booze for Joe. Henry Small remembers that when he worked for Otis during the early 1960s, Otis would get Joe bottles of "Four Roses." Small's memory is corroborated by Otis' diary: Otis mentions the stuff by name. Along with bringing alcohol to Joe, Otis also took Joe to the alcohol: "took him to North Pomfret after beer" on the first day of one summer.[25]

One might conclude that Otis Wheeler just up and decided one day to take on the responsibility of caring for Joe for the rest of his life, but it was not pure sympathy that initially encouraged Wheeler. There were practical reasons, too. At the time, Otis was still fully engaged in dairy farming at the Cabot place. One aspect of his operation was that the farm didn't have enough land for all of his cattle. Between 1961 when Otis noted Joe nine times in his diary and 1962 when he wrote about him fifty-four times, Otis made a deal with Joe to pasture some of his heifers on Joe's land. Beginning on June 14, Otis "fixed fence up to Joes" for four days in a row and then worked on it again the 21st and finished the job the next day. Two days later Otis "took hefeirs up to Joes;" there were "8 head."[26]

The cattle Otis had up to Joe Ranger's provided plenty of occasions for interaction between the two men. The day after Wheeler took his cattle up to Joe's for the first time, he went up to check on them, and probably saw Joe. He definitely saw Joe a couple days later when Joe came walking down to tell Otis that one of the heifers got out. Otis took Joe home and rounded up the truant animal. The cattle were all in the pasture on July 15th when Otis "took Joes groceries up," but two days later Joe came down again to report that the heifers were out once more. Otis again took Joe home and when he arrived found that the cows had all re-entered the pasture, so no rodeo ensued. Otis didn't take any chances, however, but got his tools and "fixed fence the rest of [the] day."[27]

Otis rewarded Joe with a six-pack of beer a couple days later for his diligence in keeping track of the cattle. Things were quiet the next week when Otis "took Joes mail up," but the week after that found "Joe down" because "2 hefiers [were] out." Otis then spent a number of days "up to Joes [to] look at hefiers" and try to find where they were getting out. He evidently found the weak spot and fixed the fence well enough to hold them for good this time. The next time Joe came down to Otis' to report on the heifers, it was because one of them had a bull calf born. Two days later, Otis "Brought [the] hefeirs home from Joes" for the winter and "caught [the] calf."[28]

For the next two years Otis continued to pasture heifers on Joe's land, with the same results as 1962. He fixed fence, took the cattle up, checked on them, thanked Joe for reporting their escapes, found new-born calves, and brought them all back home in the fall.[29]

After Otis Wheeler brought his cattle home from Joe's, he continued to go up to visit Joe and run errands for him. Getting Joe's groceries by now was a regular part of Otis' routine, but he also did other things Joe asked. In October of the first year he used Joe's land, Otis "took Joe over to" the town clerk's office in "Pomfret to pay [his property] taxes." The next fall he drove Joe over there the first week of November, and then again in 1964.[30]

Another annual rite Otis Wheeler instituted after pasturing his cattle at Joe's was taking him holiday dinners. Otis brought Thanksgiving dinners to Joe in both 1962 and 1963. Two days before Christmas in 1962 Otis went up to bring Joe a Christmas package and then on Christmas day surprised him with a plate of food from the Wheeler's dinner table. Although there is no mention of any presents the next year, Otis again brought Christmas dinner up to Joe.[31]

Otis also took on the responsibility of hauling Joe's firewood to him. Otis' diary for 1963 includes entries relating that he "drew [Joe] 2 loads wood" in May, "1 cord wood for Joe from Stetsons" on December 26th, and then the next day "drew [the] rest of Joes wood [from] Stetsons" which was "3 cords." When it was time to haul Joe's wood the next year, Otis got a load each day on November 8th and 9th, paying Ralph Stetson "for Joes" firewood. On November 11th Otis noted that Henry Small, who worked for Otis, "drew 4 loads" of wood from Stetsons' to Joes," finishing up the job.[32] Small well remembers when he "used to haul Joe's wood" as a teenager. "I was working for Otis" at the time, Small recalled, and "I used to pick it up at Buster Stetson's...and take the wood up to old Joe." Henry Small summed up what he remembered of Joe Ranger's latter years by saying that Otis "took care of Joe in a lot of ways."[33] These "ways" ensured that when Joe Ranger left this world, he and Otis Wheeler were on good terms.

Joe Ranger's end came December 2, 1964. Otis Wheeler had been up to Joe's many times that fall bringing him groceries, whisky, kerosene, his state check, and firewood without noting Joe's health. On Thanksgiving Otis took dinner up to Joe and then the next day brought him up two pounds of butter. Joe must have appeared fine, for if he had been ill, Otis would most certainly have checked on him daily over the next several days. As it was, Otis didn't go up. On December 1, Otis wrote in his diary that "Scott Harrington stopped" by to say that he had gone in to check on Joe after plowing the road and found "Joe wasn't to good."[34]

Scott Harrington's own recollection of that day vividly gives us the scene and nature of Joe's condition. Scott had been plowing out the road to Joe's that winter and whenever he got to Joe's place and got the snow pushed back and the truck turned around, Joe would appear in the doorway motioning for Scott to come in. The morning of the 1st was different, however. No smoke was coming out of Joe's chimney.

> "I got down there and plowed out and Joe didn't come to the door and I went up there and I hallowed 'Joe' and I could hear someone mumbling [inside]. [The] old dilapidated door had a hook on the inside [and it was locked]. I couldn't get in and he couldn't come to the door so I went back down to the truck and got a tire iron [and] reached through the crack [in the door] and unhitched it and I went in. Here's old Joe laying on the bunk, bran sacks and an old coat over him he was in bad shape. He'd had a shock [and I] couldn't understand a word he was saying. There was no wood in the stove - colder than a barn in there - so I got a fire going and I tried to make Joe understand that I was going to leave and I'd get somebody in there [to help him].
>
> "Well, I come back over here [to North Pomfret to see] Albert Parker [who was one of the selectmen at the time]. I told Albert, 'Somebody's got to do something about Joe. He's had a shock, he just can't do anything for himself, can't even get out of bed.' So I took off. And that day I guess they went somewhere and was going to get him into a [nursing] home. [Well, Joe] must have stayed there all that [day and the next] night. I had to go over the next morning because it snowed that night [and] I didn't know if he was there or what was going on, but there weren't no tracks in the snow where anybody had been, so I went up and the door weren't even locked. [I] opened the door and old Joe was set in the chair right in front of the stove, dead. I went right back out and stopped at Albert's again and they got him out of there.[35]

Scott Harrington recalled what he remembered about Joe's death, but there were some things he didn't know. While Albert Parker along with Moses Chase did indeed go "see about Joe Ranger," to find a place for him as Scott remembered, Joe was not left all alone from the morning Harrington found him ill to the next morning when he found him dead. Unknown to Scott, the Wheelers went up to see what they could do to help Joe. On hearing of Joe's condition, Otis must have gone right up. We don't know how Joe was when Otis got up there, but it wasn't long before Joe had recovered his senses and could speak. Otis wrote that he went to White River to get Joe "a Pint Whiskey." He wouldn't have done this for a man in the unintelligible throes of death. Otis' brother Burton also went up to Joe's that day to see what he could do and built up the fire in the stove again. That evening Burton went back home for supper and called Dr. Cusson to come up and examine Joe. At 9:00 p.m. the doctor showed up at Otis' and the Wheelers took him up to Joe's place. Dr. Cusson examined Joe and Burton remembers Joe telling the doctor, "My heart goes fast and then slow." Joe had evidently recovered enough that they left him in bed with a good fire going and would come up to see him in the morning. Burton went up the next morning around 7:00 a.m. and found Joe was up. Joe asked Burton to help him "Pull my golashes up," meaning his suspenders, and when Burton left Joe, he was sitting in his chair. There is little question that Burton Wheeler was the last person to see Joe Ranger alive.

Although we know who last saw Joe alive, several people claimed to have been the first one to find Joe dead. Out of all of them, it appears either Scott Harrington or Otis Wheeler found him. We have Scott Harrrington's memory and Otis Wheeler's diary, and they don't agree. Harrington claimed there were no previous tracks in the snow when he found Joe, but Otis Wheeler's diary claims Joe was alive at 7:00 a.m. and dead by 10:00 a.m. Either Joe was not dead when Harrington came in that morning and found him in his chair, or he is mistaken about there being no tracks in the snow and came after Burton Wheeler had been there earlier. Even to this day there is disagreement on who first found Joe Ranger dead. All agreed, however, that a character had passed on.[36]

11

Remembrance

As soon as word got out that Joe Ranger had died, people reminisced. In her weekly North Pomfret column, Irene Scott announced Joe's death with a profile of what she remembered was special about him:

"You all know by now that another old Pomfretite has left our midst. Joe Ranger - Maybe not the oldest resident, but by far the most well-known. [Joe] was known far and wide, as the Hermit of Bunker Hill. Well - Hermit or no - Joe had his own way of life and no one, despite our trying, could alter it. - I'll always remember Joe as being our first visitor on the day we moved to Pomfret fifteen years ago. And in all the years that followed, his weekly hikes to the store and back, Joe always found time to stop and sing a song, recite a poem, tell a joke or lend some good sound advice about animals and plants. I learned most of what I know about wild flowers, wild plants, herbs and bird life from Joe. He was a lover of all animal life - even to the one of many beavers in his pond, called 'Jimmy.' Believe it or not - Jimmy would surface at Joe's call, take the tidbit offered - flap his big tail several times then disappear in the deep cool water - waiting for Joe's next call. Joe's prime desire in life was to be left alone - and that is the way he died – alone - but for one old yellow cat that was found nestled in his lap."[1]

Scott highlighted all the dominant strands of Joe's character, which were "memorable." No doubt, as others heard and read of Joe's death, they also reflected upon their own experiences with him. As with Scott, it was the remarkable about Joe, that came to the forefront. Over time, these memories became articulated into the stories featured in chapter 6, which to this day, still serve as the primary vehicle for remembering Joe.

Stories of Joe Ranger were told and printed. The media helped keep the memory of Joe Ranger alive when *Associated Press* reporter Nancy Shulins wrote an article about him in July 1977.[2] While she knew of the existence of Joe's diaries, she either chose not to consult them, or did and couldn't read his handwriting. Instead of relying on documentary sources, Shulins based her article on the tales of Joe's former neighbors, primarily Otis Wheeler and his sister, Mildred Burns. As a result, we get a glimpse of how their memories were presented to the reading public.

The Wheelers remembered Joe in more positive terms than they expressed when he was alive. We have seen the struggles Otis Wheeler had with Joe Ranger and that relations between them were not always good, but in death, and to Shulins, Joe was discussed with special reverence. Otis did "admit reluctantly" that Joe could be mean, telling Shulins one version of the story of Joe and Albert Parker's melon patch, but Wheeler termed himself Joe's "best friend" and told about the time Joe came in the middle of the night to plant two maple trees in Otis' yard "as a present."[3]

Otis' sister, Mildred's stories also recalled Joe fondly. She shuddered when she described to Shulins the mess at Joe's place and how he let his cats clean his dinner plate. No doubt, Burns had once been disgusted by Joe's lack of hygiene, but now, separated from Joe by time and death, Burns made light of Joe's filth. "My I miss him," she told Shulins.[4] In missing Joe sympathetically, his friends and neighbors and acquaintances altered, or at least adjusted their memories to reflect upon him, and themselves, as the occasion warranted.

The Wheelers presented Joe as they *wanted* to remember him because they didn't have to deal with him directly anymore. Nancy Shulins took down the Wheeler's stories verbatim, but because she was a reporter needing to fashion a story herself, she added to what she was told, slightly altering what was widely understood about Joe locally. In essence, Joe's neighbors remembered him for an "audience" who then presented their stories through the prism of her understanding and her need to tell an interesting, articulated story for her own newspaper audience. As a result, some new themes were introduced into the lore as coming from memory.[5]

The story Shulins told of Joe Ranger identified him as "a penniless French-Canadian Indian." The construct of Joe as penniless was mostly true, but painting him as a French Canadian ignores the fact that his mother was a Yankee and that he was in fact native to the area, as he died only a few miles from where he was born. While he did claim an Indian ancestor, Joe and his progenitor were generations apart. Some have pointed to his connection with nature as a legacy of this native connection, but this is silly, and says more about those making the claim than it does about Joe.[6]

Along with fixing Joe's ethnicity and heritage, Shulins made it seem like Joe had lived in filth ever since he "bought his homestead in 1911," instead of the reality of his slow decline into slovenliness as his poverty deepened between the 1920s and 1950s. She even made poverty sound like fun: "When he wasn't mowing hay with a scythe, telling stories or tending his garden, Ranger sat in the fields and sang to the cows [and when] the work was done, he joined residents who brought their picnics to Joe Ranger Road" for an outing in his pasture, as if Joe's was the epitome of a pastoral idyllic life.[7]

Not only was Joe's life idealized, so was his death. According to

Shulins, Joe died without suffering. On the night he died, she wrote, "Ranger lit the potbellied stove and sat in his chair with his cat for the last time."[8] Not mentioned was the fact that he had died a messy death, lingering with inadequate care before finally expiring. In short, Nancy Shulins passed off her article about Joe as if it was a declaration of truth instead of the selective and invented tale it actually was.

Nancy Shulins was one among many who fashioned narratives of Joe Ranger based on selective memory. While the facts of filth, wit, and oddness stand out as dominant themes for most who remember Joe, a few people's remembrances transcend mere episodic encounters. We will explore these later.

Joe Ranger was such a significant character to people that many wanted something of his to remember him by. Folks were selective, however. They did not seek out *all* the accoutrements that made Joe

Josephine Dupuis and the birdcage she salvaged from Joe Ranger's after his death. Photo by the author.

such a distinctive character. Dirty clothes and food-encrusted plates were of no interest to anyone. Instead, people looked for anything interesting, beautiful, or practical that Joe had owned. Otis Wheeler took Joe's diaries. Albert Dutton ended up with some of his books. Burton Wheeler found a pure white dish in the shape of a setting hen. Josephine Dupuis found a beautiful old-fashioned birdcage. And Walt Howard's son, Steve, found a decent chair. Who knows what else was taken. Items that had been unused and covered up for over fifty years were actually quite nice.[9]

In addition to objects from his house, the natural wonders Joe lived with were also uprooted and taken. The berry plants were dug up and replanted in backyards throughout the region. The flowers Joe raised were also transplanted. An attempt was made to box up and move the bees inhabiting the house walls in order to establish a workable beehive. And the beaver living in the pond were soon trapped, skinned, and sold by one of the local youths. It didn't take long for the property to be stripped of all vestiges of Joe Ranger.[10]

People attached meanings to all the things they took away from Joe's place. The story of what happened to his woodstove illustrates how meaning developed. Originally taken as a useful item, the stove was later transformed into a museum piece dedicated to the memory of one of Vermont's unique characters.

Joe's stove was not taken by the memento seekers who descended upon his house after he died. It sat there undisturbed throughout the rest of the winter, the next spring, summer, and throughout the fall. Once cold weather came again, however, it was taken by someone who never knew Joe Ranger and only wanted to keep warm.

Carl Johnson set up Joe's old stove in his house in December 1965. Johnson had come from Massachusetts and purchased and moved into the former Handy house in West Hartford that spring. He had been hired to teach mechanical drawing at Hartford High

School and had looked around the area for some time before settling on the Handy place.

How Carl Johnson ended up with Joe Ranger's stove was due to Johnson's dry cleaner, Burt Wheeler. Johnson would chat with Wheeler when he stopped at Wheeler's shop to drop off and pick up his laundry. One day Johnson mentioned to Burt that he was looking for a used woodstove. Right then and there, Wheeler told Johnson he knew of a stove he could have. Years later, Carl Johnson recalled Burt's description. He said the stove was up in an old abandoned house that used to belong to an old fellow who lived all alone.[11] "He's dead, he doesn't need it," Wheeler told him. On December 9th, Burt

Joe Ranger's stove as displayed at the Hartford Historical Society's Garipay House. Photo by the author.

and brother Otis "got [the] stove from Joes" for Johnson.12 In a matter of days it was warming Johnson's home.

The Johnsons used Joe Ranger's old stove all the time they lived in the Handy place, and then again after Carl sold the house and set up a mobile home nearby. A number of years passed before Johnson replaced the trailer with a house and after using Joe's stove a year or so there, Johnson decided to purchase a new, efficient woodstove. The old stove was relegated to the barn. Here it stayed until a chance conversation between Johnson and Hartford Historical Society archivist, Pat Stark, changed its fate.13

Johnson and Stark both worked for the town of Hartford in the late 1990s. He was a part-time lister, and she was the listers' assistant. Stark sometimes spoke of items and issues relating to her work with the Hartford Historical Society. One day the two of them were reminiscing about old former residents of the area. Joe Ranger came up in their conversation and Johnson mentioned that he had Joe Ranger's old Glenwood stove. Pointing out that it was just in his barn collecting dust, Johnson asked if the Historical Society would be interested in having it donated to them to display in their exhibition space at the Garipy House the Society owned in Hartford Village. Stark jumped at the opportunity to acquire something belonging to Joe Ranger, and secured the stove for the Society. Soon it was on display, garnished by Hanson Carroll's photographs and stories about Joe.14

This story of Joe Ranger's stove highlights how it became an icon, simply because it was owned by him. Neither Pat Stark nor Carl Johnson had ever met Joe Ranger. But they both came to recognize his popularity. Pat Stark came about it quite naturally. She had family who knew stories about old Joe. She had heard about him and knew he was a "local character." Also, being the archivist for the Hartford Historical Society primed her to keep a lookout for artifacts associated with people of local significance to add to the Society's col-

181

lection. Thus it is easy to understand Stark's interest in saving the old stove.[15]

Carl Johnson's interest in Joe Ranger's stove as a relic developed slowly, over time. Initially, he knew nothing about Joe. Johnson was no romantic. He came to the area to teach high school, not to learn about local characters. Once settled in his West Hartford home, however, Johnson began to learn about his neighbors and the dynamics of this small village and rural neighborhood. Although he was considered a curmudgeon by some, Carl Johnson's encounters with the peo-

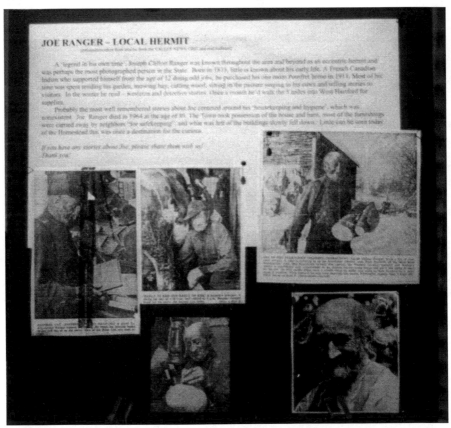

Display accompanying Joe Ranger's stove at the Hartford Historical Society's Garipay House. Photo by the author.

ple of West Hartford over the years at the post office and store resulted in his growing appreciation for the village's "old timers."

One was Allen Chadwick, or "Chaddy," who lived in West
Hartford and was somewhat Joe Ranger's heir. Chaddy had grown
up in the area, never married, rarely washed, and lived in an old
shack on the road between West Hartford and North Pomfret. There
was also Irving Neil, who lived across the road from Chaddy. Neil
was widowed and washed, but he was noted for living with a multitude of cats who sat all around, and on him when he relaxed out on
his front porch evenings. Neil also had an excellent berry patch.
Thinking back about Chaddy and Neil years later, Johnson claimed
that he was impressed by their persistence and independence in the
face of poverty. Neither one had ever looked for a handout.

Reminiscing about West Hartford's old timers, Johnson gave the
impression of being impervious to the efforts to glorify these men
because they were "characters."[16] Maybe this was so. However, there
was a reason Carl Johnson gave Joe Ranger's stove to the Hartford
Historical Society when he did. His memories of the Wheelers, the
stories of Joe, the dead old timers, and the stove he had down in his
barn, were all rekindled in the early 1990s by a series of articles
appearing in the local newspapers that featured Joe Ranger. Reading
these articles helped set the stage for Johnson's donation of Joe's stove
to the Hartford Historical Society, and at the same time, provided
people with a larger meaning to attach to Joe Ranger's memory. The
final chapter will explore why these articles resonated with so many
people.

12

Legacy

The most visible evidence of Joe Ranger's legacy is the road named for him. After Joe's death, those who had known him continued to refer to the dirt road from the Quechee-West Hartford Road to Bunker Hill by the name of its most famous former resident. Over the years, even those who were unfamiliar with Joe learned the road's colloquial designation. In time, the towns of Hartford and Pomfret each officially recognized the cross-border road with road signs: Joe Ranger Road.

Traveling that stretch, folks continued to experience a part of what they remembered or imagined Joe's world to have encompassed. They passed the Cabot place where Otis Wheeler lived, went past the former Brockway place the Marshalls owned, past open fields and pastures, past the old Udall orchard and barn, past Joe's dilapidated house and the beaver pond, and up the hill to Albert Parker's former home where the road intersects with the one leading down to North Pomfret. Even though former residents and many of the buildings were gone, enough of the old persisted along Joe Ranger Road to maintain the sense that one just might meet up with Joe himself, making his way home.

The subsequent history of Joe Ranger Road, however, made clear that Joe Ranger's world was indeed gone. The era of farming had passed and it was replaced by an extended period of contest over what was to follow. Between Joe's death in 1964 and the early 1990s, several plans were put forward for developing Joe Ranger Road. And, as with Joe's own best-laid plans, these also did not come to fruition.

What to do with Joe's property was the first scene of conflict. When Joe died in late 1964, he was indebted to two entities: the town of Pomfret and the State of Vermont. At his death, he owed Pomfret for back taxes. Joe's property taxes from 1937 through 1953 had never been paid. He also had never repaid the mortgage he had given the town back in 1922. At that time, Joe mortgaged his farm to the town for $345 as a guarantee that the cost of caring for his mother would eventually be met. Since he had never paid off the mortgage, interest on the original debt had accumulated so that at his death, the total amount due had ballooned to $903.90.[1]

Joe was also indebted to the State of Vermont. In 1949, when Joe began receiving old-age assistance, the commissioner of the Vermont Department of Social Welfare put a lien against his property so the State could reclaim the money it paid out to Joe during his life by taking its share out of whatever his property sold for after his death. It didn't work out that way, however. Joe's estate was insolvent. His estate owed the town $274.39 for back taxes, and, according to a note from the Department of Social Welfare, the estate owed the State $9,040.00 for the old-age assistance Joe had received plus the expenses of his funeral which the State also had paid. Regardless of the amount the State said it was owed, when Ric Davis was appointed administrator of Joe's estate in February 1965, he claimed in his statement to the Probate Court that the "amount of debts due from said deceased is $5,000." Davis included $100 to pay himself for administering the estate, bringing the total to $5,100.

Davis then deducted the value of Joe's personal estate, $420.28, from the debts and came up with a bill of $4,679.72 the estate owed. In order to pay the debts, Davis petitioned the court for permission to sell "All and the same deeded to Joseph C Ranger by Frank F Howard dated May 11 1911 recorded in Book 21 page 215 [of the] Pomfret Land Records." A license to sell the property was then duly granted Davis in April. At that point, the land should have been sold and whatever it sold for, divided between the town of Pomfret and the State. But this did not happen. In all likelihood, if Joe's place had been sold at public auction, it would have brought much less than what was owed the town and State.[2]

Given the prospect of not getting fully reimbursed from Joe's estate if the property was sold, Ric Davis, the town of Pomfret, and the State of Vermont got together to work out an agreement so that all parties concerned would be compensated. Instead of selling Joe's place for whatever they could get for it, the town and State each got part of Joe's property.

In dividing Joe's land and keeping title to it, the two parties were able to satisfy the debts owed them without creating new costs in the process. Holding onto their part of Joe's place made economic sense to Pomfret's leaders, who recognized that if they sold their part of the Ranger land, it would cost the town much more in the long run than the $903.90 and $274.39 they would have received for the old mortgage and the back taxes.

For if the town sold Joe's place, it was quite possible someone might actually establish a modern home there. If that happened, the town would have to continue to maintain and plow the old road, and in addition, if there were kids in the household, the town would also have to educate the children and transport them to school. With that expensive prospect looming over the sale of Joe's property, town officials decided it didn't make sense to sell it.[3]

Before the final decision to not sell Joe's place was made, however, the town had already solicited bids for it. And several came in. One was from Larry Page. Page lived in Hartland near Walt Howard's home. He and Howard both worked at the Goodyear plant in Windsor and Larry used to ride back and forth with Walt. Page had met Joe Ranger and was familiar with his place because he used to hunt deer up on the Howard land surrounding Joe's. Through hunting, Page got to know the area, walking the hills and valleys that Walt's family owned. He also got to know Joe. Like many hunters, Page stopped in to see Joe during deer season.

Because he knew Joe and liked the area where he lived, when Page found out that Pomfret had ended up with most of the property and was planning to sell it, he decided to bid for it. It is not known how Page felt about Joe and the property. Did he want to buy the land in part because it had belonged to Joe? Did he find the lay of the land and it's seclusion appealing? Did he imagine building a house and moving to the property? Or did Page just see a chance to pick up a piece of land, cheap? Larry Page is no longer alive, so we will never really know. However, we do know he wanted the place. Walt Howard remembered talking with Page about Joe's property and asking Page about his bid. Page was disappointed, saying that the town had decided not to sell the place after all. He wasn't sure why, but we know.[4]

On April 15, 1966, when Ric Davis deeded the bulk of Joe's property to the town of Pomfret, he also deeded 6.1 acres to the State of Vermont. It was probably Davis' sister, Irene Scott, infatuated with the memory of Joe and his beaver, who wished there was some way of preserving Joe's beaver ponds as a memorial to his life. An idea was then hatched that solved the problem of reimbursing the State for the money Joe's estate owed. Why not turn the ponds and the lands around it into a small state park or preserve dedicated to Joe?

We don't know the details of the negotiations between Davis and state officials, but a deal was made. Although it wasn't turned into a park, the Vermont Fish and Game Department accepted the land "to eventually develop a small impoundment for a cold water fishery" and to encourage waterfowl habitat. When the land was deeded to the Fish and Game Department, it was assigned a value of $10,800, enough to cover the amount owed the state. Although this figure overvalued the parcel significantly, accepting it allowed officials to play with the accounting so the debt of Joe Ranger's estate to the State of Vermont could be erased.[5]

After these transactions took place the town and State essentially left Joe's land as it was deeded to them. Years later, the town gave permission to the volunteer fire department to burn down Joe's house as a training seminar for its members. The night before the scheduled training was to take place, however, someone snuck over and set it on fire. The training session was postponed.[6]

Pomfret figured it would make Joe's place pay by using it. Town officials turned it into a stump dump. The old cellar hole was filled in, an area up back was leveled off, and refuse began being hauled in. It didn't take long for stumps, brush, and rotten logs to accumulate and ironically make more of a mess of the area than Joe Ranger ever had.[7]

Across the road, the State of Vermont made plans to develop Joe's ponds as a part of their fishery efforts. For the project to go ahead, more land surrounding the original parcel was needed. Research determined that the Howard family owned the adjoining land. Officials approached Ralph Howard about the possibility of deeding the Fish and Game Department some of the land he and his late brother had owned near the pond as part of the effort. Ralph was willing. All that was needed was to make out the paperwork and he would sign it. Ralph died, however, before the deeds could be signed.[8]

Ralph Howard's death did not end the effort by the State to acquire his former land around the pond. But the plans of Ralph's nephew, John, for the family property did. The trout ponds did not materialize. Instead, John Howard ended up with all of the land his uncle and father had owned together. His sale of this land to a developer in 1969 set the stage for a fight involving more than just town officials trying to keep one house from being built on Joe Ranger Road.[9]

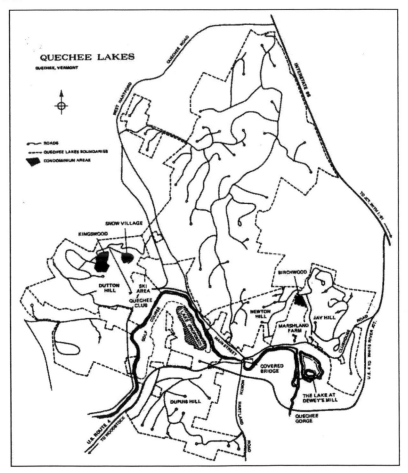

Plan of Quechee Lakes Development, Quechee, Vermont. From John St. Croix, Historical Highlights of the Town of Harford, Vermont.

The town of Pomfret easily succeeded in keeping Joe's place from being built upon by simply keeping it as town property. However, the town didn't own the old Howard land surrounding Joe's lot. In the early 1970s, officials and concerned local folks fought and won a hard battle to keep the Quechee Lakes Corporation from expanding its Quechee village development into Pomfret on the former Howard lands.

John Howard sold all his family's Pomfret land to Quechee Lakes after giving up farming in the late 1960s. At the time, Howard faced the need to upgrade his old barn to comply with regulations if he was to continue. His brother, Walt, offered to help build a milking parlor if John wanted to keep on farming, but John said no. Profits were elusive, and he was sick of beating his head against the wall trying to get by. So, he sold his cows and quit farming. Not long afterward Quechee Lakes offered him $60,000 for the Pomfret land and the Thomas lot in Hartford. John took the money and later went to work for the corporation.[10]

Before Quechee Lakes' purchase of Howard's land in Joe Ranger's old neighborhood, Pomfret had never experienced any sort of major development. Pomfret was a Vermont success story. The town was still a patchwork of forests and fields, natives continued to live in town, and newcomers owned and maintained the old homes and barns. Natives worked the land while newcomers footed the bill, all the while maintaining the classic image of a serene Vermont rural community. Quechee Lakes' plans for hundreds of new second-homes on one-acre lots did not fit in with Pomfret's self-image.[11]

Quechee Lakes' plans couldn't have come at a worse time for a land development company in Vermont. Throughout the 1960s, as Vermont attracted more and more people to the state, the negative aspects of growth came to the forefront. Some felt Vermont was a victim of its own success. The state had succeeded in fighting rural poverty and promoting itself as a place of rest and relaxation, but the campaign to attract newcomers worked too well, many believed. People had effectively resettled the old farms and many of the villages. The problem was that more people kept coming. Governor Deane Davis put it succinctly in 1969 when he said, "Once you had to...get any kind of development for Vermont[,] now our economy has progressed to the point where the major effort must be devoted to slowing it down."[12]

When the people of Pomfret learned about Quechee Lakes' plans to expand, they mobilized to keep the company from developing in town. The most concerned citizens all lived in the eastern part of town and closest to the proposed development. Their ranks included those who had moved to Pomfret for the rural atmosphere. The Coogans, Marshalls, St. Johns, Baileys, Andersons, and Gratiots all felt under siege and reacted accordingly.

An intense effort was mounted to instate zoning regulation in order to stymie Quechee Lakes' plans. Through newsletters, meetings, and forums, enough residents were convinced to vote for the proposed new rules at a special Town Meeting in May 1972, and opponents of Quechee Lakes heralded that the development plans were dead.

Under the new ordinance, according to *The Vermont Standard* reporter covering the meeting, "two-acre plots are required for all houses, with [the] entire town zoned rural residential. No matter how large the parcel of land no more than two homes can be built for commercial purposes within a two year period." Ending his report, he added, "It appears Pomfret has come up with a timely and effective zoning ordinance."[13]

Quechee Lakes' plans for Pomfret were defeated. Developing only two lots every two years was not the company's idea of a successful project. Instead, the company held onto the Howard land for years without moving to develop it. The battle over developing Joe's neighborhood now a thing of the past, the reprinting of the 1977 Associated Press article on Joe Ranger in the unofficial Quechee Lakes' newspaper, *The Quechee Times*, seemed to signal that the fight for Joe Ranger Road was over. In fact, it had only begun.[14]

While Quechee Lakes' plans for the former Howard property on Joe Ranger Road in the early 1970s were defeated, the 1980s found a renewed interest in developing the area, and set the stage for reviving the memory of Joe. Pomfret Associates, a group of investors with absolutely no connection to Pomfret, bought Quechee Lakes' Pomfret holdings in 1980 and eventually succeeded in subdividing the property for development. Whereas Quechee Lakes had failed to subdivide the Howard land because Pomfret's zoning regulations prevented it from doing so, Pomfret Associates succeeded by working within the established regulations.

Pomfret Associates went through the town's application process for subdivision, adjusted their original plans to meet regulatory requirements, and planned for a gradual development of their property. The plans included subdividing the 430 acres into twenty-four lots. Twenty-one of the lots were for high-end housesites, while three lots totaling 155 acres, including the fields of the old Udall place, were granted to the Ottaquechee Land Trust to be preserved as open space.

Although there was plenty of local opposition, it only delayed the inevitable. People spoke out at meetings and tried to block the extension of electricity to the development site, but the planners of the project had done what was necessary to pass muster with town and state regulations.

With imminent change for Joe Ranger's old neighborhood about to take place, those living nearby and those who were familiar with the area resigned themselves to the fact. Although folks had to endure

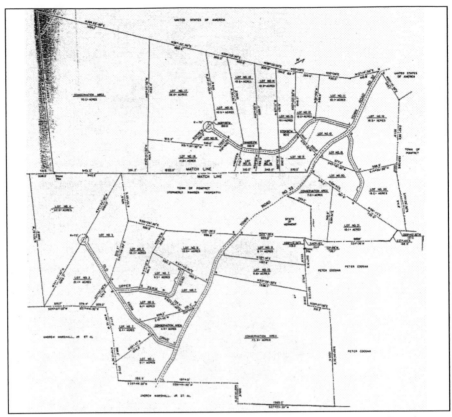

Subdivision of the former Howard land in Pomfret, Vermont by Pomfret
Associates. Pomfret, Vermont Town Clerk's Office.

what was about to happen to this piece of paradise, they wanted to
express their recognition that a special piece of rural Vermont was
changing forever.

These expressions revived the memory of Joe Ranger as a way to
mark the upcoming changes. By contrasting Joe's happy life of poverty with the current acquisitive, materialistic culture represented by
Pomfret Associates' proposed upscale development, people were
meant to understand the importance of maintaining a rural agricultural image to keeping Vermont the special place so many believed it
to be.

194

A variety of people highlighted Joe in the media during the late 1980s and early 1990s before the development got under way. In January 1987, Herman Lindemann, a Pomfret resident who lived on the Old King's Highway and worked for *The Vermont Standard*, wrote his piece: "Memory Of Joe Ranger Lives On." The next month, Jim Kenyon included Joe Ranger in his article about Otis Wheeler's move out of the neighborhood. A couple years later, *Valley News* correspondent, Andrea Heil, wrote about "The Man Who Lived On Joe Ranger Road." Collamer Abbott, in the "Vermont Past" section of the *Green Mountain Gazette*, noted "The Man Who Talked To Beavers." And Will and Jane Curtis did a piece on "Joe Ranger" for their radio series, "The Nature of Things."[15]

Herman Lindemann used Nancy Shulins' 1977 article about Joe Ranger as a starting point for his own article on Joe, but he also visited with the Wheelers and did a little research on his own. While the result was a mix of fact and fiction, Lindemann successfully conveyed a sense of Joe as a special old timer. At the end of his article, Lindemann expressed his anti-development position by concluding that whatever Joe's "eccentricities, it is undeniable that in some small way he left his mark on this little corner of Vermont. Joe Ranger Road has no housing developments, as yet. Indeed, barely a house stands on the road." Pushing the point home, Lindemann proclaimed that "Joe Ranger would have liked that."[16]

Like Herman Lindemann, all the others who revived Joe did so while bemoaning the present-day changes. Jim Kenyon portrayed Otis Wheeler as the last of the old timers in his article, but he also identified Joe Ranger as the original old timer of the neighborhood, "for whom the road leading up the hill [from Wheelers] is named." Joe had been a "local institution," so with the imminent changes due to development, local characters and institutions would be a thing of the past.[17]

Andrea Heil, who worked at the *Valley News* with Jim Kenyon, was sent out in May 1990 to research and write a piece about Joe Ranger, but also to discuses the changes about to take place, as contractors right then were widening Joe Ranger Road. With former stories in hand, Heil spoke with the Wheelers and related the conventional Joe Ranger story line, but she also captured some new stories after inter- viewing Hartford's Town Manager, Ralph Lehman, who had encoun- tered Ranger in the 1950s.

In the middle of her article, Heil set the stage for the thrust of the story: change. She described what was left of Joe's home as "a crum- bling foundation" and described Joe Ranger Road as "bumpy and rutted in spots, and unplowed in the winter." That was part of what made the area special, however, because it was "an inviting country road with an old white farmhouse at one end and a beaver pond at the other. Lined with stone walls and big maple trees and white and gray birch, the road has views of faraway pastures and silos shining in the sun." Heil's description was the epitome of the rural Vermont image everyone had loved and worked to maintain.[18]

While the area was beautiful, scenic, and somewhat agricultural at the present, "a development of 20 high-priced dwellings (with an average lot size of 20 acres) is planned," wrote Heil, adding, "and work is in progress." She then gave a short history of the develop- ment plans and gave the developers credit for planning to "maintain the scenic nature of the road...without mowing down all of the old maples and the stone wall." That was the only credit she offered, however, for she quickly changed gears, making the point that the development was viewed negatively when she quoted Otis Wheeler's sister, Hertha, saying, "That little road isn't going to be the same" when the developers got done with it. Heil then reported that "the road's imminent change is also unsettling for Kye Cochran and her husband Ron Pogue, who live on Joe Ranger Road in a farmhouse that once belonged to Cochran's grandparents," the Cabots. After relating Cochran's memories of Joe, Heil described Joe's diaries, which Cochran possessed at the time, and presented Hertha Wheeler's account of the naming of Joe Ranger Road, before ending with Lehman's assertion that "They named [the road] after [Joe] because he lived there all his life."[19]

Others had spread the word about the impending changes to Joe Ranger's old neighborhood, but Will and Jane Curtis brought the drama to its logical conlusion: What had been, was now gone. After leaving the West Hartford farm for a larger one in Hartland, Vermont, Will Curtis entered the Vermont Legislature and later began a completely new endeavor as a naturalist, producing commentaries through Vermont Public Radio for national distribution, before retiring to Woodstock village.[20]

At the time of the ongoing construction on Joe Ranger Road, Will and Jane Curtis decided to present their own memories of Joe Ranger in juxtaposition with the current project on his road. Ranger was "a little gnome of a man" who "used to stride down the road past our farm every two weeks or so," according to Jane, and "over his shoulder he'd have a stick with a bandanna tied on the end...going for groceries." Joe didn't need many store-bought goods, however, for "Joe was pretty self-sufficient."[21]

Stessing Ranger's simple lifestyle, Jane Curtis continued:

> Sometimes in the summer we'd hike up to visit with Joe; he was a pleasant man and liked company in moderation. As I said, he was self-sufficient. He invited us inside his dwelling to show us his living arrangements. The only furniture was one chair in the middle of the room next to a wood stove. Everything was very efficient. He kept a pile of wood at hand, and around the edge of the room was his store of potatoes. When he wanted sweetening, he just reached in through a hole in the wall and fetched out a fistful of honey, courtesy of the bees who shared the house with him.

197

All he needed to buy was some coffee and tinned meat. What kept him so spry, he claimed, was that he hadn't had to eat 'no danged woman's cookin.' 22

The Curtises' fanciful account of Joe continued until the last two sentences of their 470-word commentary when the present abruptly intruded. Joe Ranger had passed on, never to return, as had the life of simplicity he had lived: "Joe's house has been bulldozed away, the beaver evicted, and rows of condominiums now surround a neat pond. The paved road is called Joe Ranger Drive." It didn't matter that Joe's house had been burned by pranksters, that beaver had returned to the old pond, that only one new house had been built so far, that the road was still dirt, and that it remained Joe Ranger Road; the Curtises had persuasively presented a dichotomy of extremes between old timers and newcomers, between what Vermont once had and what it had lost, between what it once was and what it was now.23

Former newspaperman Collamer Abbott also wrote about Joe in the summer of 1990. Abbott occasionally provided material for the small *Green Mountain Gazette* (put out by Janice Aitken, another former *Valley News* employee) and when he learned of the project for Joe Ranger Road, he sat down and set pen to paper. Over the years, Abbott had explored many of the region's back roads and he liked the Bunker Hill-Joe Ranger Road-King's Highway area of Pomfret.24

Abbott recalled his one and only encounter with Joe Ranger back in the 1950s, when Abbott was sent out to report on Joe talking to beaver for the *Valley News*. While he had found nothing to write about back then, he had plenty now. The draft Abbott sent to Aitken, led off with the current concern: "So they're going to develop the Pomfret stretch of Joe Ranger Road? Twenty twenty-acre lots on four hundred acres that once contained four farms." Abbott then recalled his skepticism about Joe's ability to call up wild beaver at will, which was confirmed when he and Joe went out to the pond and the beaver didn't come.[25]

However, Abbott ended his account with the observation that, "Now, thirty-odd years later, with Joe's Garden of Eden succumbing to a modern development," his "skepticism over these years has been eroded away." Collamer Abbott, the practical, factual, Yankee, admitted that he had eventually succumbed to the Joe Ranger myth, and the myth about rural Vermont, observing that "Maybe Joe COULD talk to Billy beaver...because, it seems to me that eventually all of us, figuratively, 'talk to beavers.'" Abbott had decided that the making and telling of myths, and the celebration of special Vermont characters like Joe Ranger was "a way of surviving" in a world of constant change. He could have added that myth making and celebration can, on occasion, also lead to change as we have seen in the case of Vermont.[26]

Epilogue

Pomfret Associates sold their holdings to a group of investors who managed to build only one house off Joe Ranger Road before internal corruption wracked the enterprise, sending one member to prison and ending any development by that group. The parcel remained untouched for the rest of the 1990s before being sold to another developer with a new variation on an old theme: He plans a development of upscale houses. The number of homes has been reduced, this time there will be no more than five. He has consolidated formerly subdivided lots, deeded more development rights to a land trust, and is planning to construct the second house soon. Joe Ranger's former house site remains vacant, still owned by the town of Pomfret.

Stories continue to be told about Joe and while those who knew him personally are diminishing yearly, a new generation picks up the narratives, retelling and adapting them for a modern-day audience with varying results. Joe's reputation as an oddity and a wit continues to be strong, but new tales recasting him as a "Mountain Man" and even as the brother of the "Lone Ranger" have also been fabricated and told to children in the area.

Along with the old and new stories about Joe, his image can still be seen in the photos many have lovingly kept over the years as valued keepsakes and constant reminders of their famous neighbor. One woman had her family's picture of Joe professionally matted and framed as a present to her parents. It hangs in their living room to this day. Another photo sits inside the birdcage one neighbor scavenged from Joe's house and displays in her home, with Joe peering through the bars, smiling as if he was a jailbird about ready to make his escape. His face has even been permanently embedded on coffee mugs in a somewhat entrepreneurial venture by one of his admirers. Joe Ranger's memory is preserved in his old neighborhood and environs.

While Joe is still celebrated locally, his wider significance has receded. In fact, Fred Tuttle notwithstanding, the era of the Vermont character has passed. Although Joe and his ilk were useful and popular as attractions between the 1930s and 1990s, they are no longer needed. They were popular during an era when witty, old, Vermont farmers served as one of the pillars of the Vermont image. Their use in a decades-old campaign to attract urban professionals proved entertaining, and useful.

The demise of Vermonters born before the 1910s who had farmed, known hard times, and viewed life with stubborn resignation naturally occurred as they aged and died off, one by one. And while old men are made every day, the passing of Joe Ranger's generation has coincided with the widespread realization that Vermont has succeeded splendidly in attracting newcomers to come and settle within its borders. With the steady decline of traditional dairy farming and the culture it sustained, modern-day newcomers to the state are infrequently exposed to the character of native farmers or native farm characters. Instead of old, white, Yankee, men, the contributions of women, Native Americans, African Americans, and immigrant groups are justly celebrated for their place in the story of the making of Vermont.

So, in the end, what are we to make of Joe Ranger's ironic life of poverty and fame? On the neighborhood stage and beyond, Joe played his part. He lived, worked with, and entertained those around him. Initially an example of what kind of person not to become, Joe then played his natural self masterfully to a rapt audience primed to pay attention to an oddity like him. He loved the attention. We have seen how he was eager for company, and connecting with people, proved to be the most satisfying benefit of Joe's life as a character.

While Joe Ranger became one of Vermont's best-known characters, on a practical level, becoming a Vermont character didn't do much for Joe. He received attention for his newfound fame, but he didn't benefit monetarily. He stayed the same, seemingly untouched by the progress around him. Many people believe this was how Joe wanted it, but we have seen that earlier in his life, Joe strove for the material things of this world. He wanted to be a successful farmer but never became one. In reality, it was Joe Ranger's failure and life of struggle that set the parameters for his fame. His story is not one of fame in spite of poverty, it is one of fame *because* of poverty. Joe's experience is an example of what can happen when local lore and official myth making intersect. And, while Vermont was reaping the seeds of success, Joe Ranger died alone, poor, and without adequate care at the height of his popularity.

Acknowledgements

Producing anything incurs debts. Writing a book adds its own special set of debts to pay. Luckily, I have lots of them. First of all I want to thank everyone who has shared with me their memories and stories about Joe Ranger. While some felt they had little to contribute, I found no piece of information about Joe unimportant while I was researching. I thank them collectively here and individually acknowledge their central role in creating this story within the notes.

Thanks are also due to other individuals who provided me with assistance in their various capacities, including: Hartford, Vermont town clerk, Mary "Beth" Hill, former Pomfret, Vermont town clerk, Hazel Harrington, and present town clerk Joann Webb for providing me with research space and access to the voluminous town records in their care. Kate Schall of the Quechee Library assisted with inter-library loans. Paul Carnahan at the Vermont Historical Society Library and the staff at the Rauner Special Collections Library at Dartmouth College provided materials from their respective repositories, as did those at the Hartford Historical Society, the Pomfret Historical Society, and the Woodstock Historical Society.

Special thanks are due to four individuals. First, I want to thank Collamer Abbot, who finally agreed that Joe Ranger was noteworthy enough to write about. While sharing his own story about Joe, Collamer also has shared his time by reading multiple drafts of this book and providing feedback.

Alan Berolzheimer never lost faith in this project, even during the times when I almost had. He has proved an expert editor, helping to shape this work and saving me from many embarrassments. Of course, any remaining mistakes are my own.

John Lutz has been an enthusiastic supporter of getting Joe Ranger's story before the public eye. He is responsible for the layout of this book and assisting in its publication. His expertise is greatly appreciated.

And finally, I thank Jere Daniell. Almost twenty years ago I walked into his office at Dartmouth College as a local with a limited education and said I was interested in history. Jere took the time to sit and talk, and invited me to come back again if I wished. I haven't stopped coming. If this book effectively communicates something, it is because of Jere. He has read almost everything I have ever written and knows just how to balance sharp criticism with insightful encouragement. His patience and generosity are unmatchable.

Notes

Chapter 1

1 Hartford, Vermont birth records, 2:17. *United States Census, Manuscript Returns for Windsor County, Vermont, 1870*, hereafter cited as *U.S. Census*. G. A. Cheney, *Glimpses Of The White River Valley, Vermont: West Hartford, Sharon, South Royalton, Royalton* (n.p. n.d.), 16-18.

2 William Bradford, *Of Plymouth Plantation 1620-1647*, Samuel Eliot Morison, ed. (New York: Alfred A. Knopf, 1952), 252-3. Jackson Turner Main, *Society And Economy In Colonial Connecticut* (Princeton: Princeton University Press, 1985), 200-234. Charles E. Clark, *The Eastern Frontier* (Hanover: University Press of New England, 1970, reprint 1985), 169-179. Alan Taylor, *Liberty Men and Great Proprietors* (Chapel Hill: The University of North Carolina Press, 1990), 62-66. Harold Fisher Wilson, *The Hill Country of Northern New England* (New York: Columbia University Press, 1936), 24-26, hereafter cited as Wilson. Henry H. Vail, *Pomfret Vermont* (Boston: Cockayne, 1930), 1:145-146, hereafter cited as Vail.

3 Harold A. Meeks, "An Isochronic Map of Vermont Settlement," *Vermont History* 38 (Spring 1970), 95-102. There were only six grants of unchartered lands in Vermont given after 1791. Of the unpreviously granted land remaining in Vermont after 1791 only Duncansborough, North and South Jay, Johnson, and Sheffield were town-size grants to groups of proprietors. Most of the rest were gores of land ranging from a few hundred to 12,000 acres. *State Papers of Vermont, Vol. II Vermont Charters*, Harry A. Black, Sec. Of State (1922), 6-7, 12-14, 58, 62-64, 71-72, 79-83, 85-87, 92-93, 108-113, 116-117, 120-121, 134-135, 141-143, 154-156, 172-174, 183-184, 188-190, 219-221.

207

4 Vermont's rural population peaked in the 1830s, *U.S. Census. Map of Windsor County, Vermont, from actual surveys by Hosea Doton, with 26 insets of villages and 10 engravings* (n.p.: 1855), hereafter cited as 1855 Atlas.

5 Ibid. *Pomfret, Vermont Land Records* 1:235; 5:250; 10:201, 298, 300; 12:525; 13:199; 14:369, 371-372, 507; 15:408; 16:382; 18/310-311; 20:331, hereafter cited as PLR. Vail, 1:107; 2:381-883, 516-517. *Vermont Agricultural Census, 1870.* Wilson, 85-89.

6 Cameron K. Clifford, "A Tale of Two Villages: The Transformation of West Hartford and North Pomfret During the Railroad Era 1845-1915, *Hartford Historical Society Quarterly* Vol. 9, Issue 3 (September 1996), 3-9, hereafter cited as Clifford. William Howard Tucker, *History of Hartford, Vermont* (Burlington: The Free Press Association, 1889), 22-23, 117-119, hereafter cited as Tucker.

7 Robert C. Jones, *The Central Vermont Railway* (Silverton, Colorado: Sundance Publications Limited, 1981), 6, 11-30. Clifford, 3-9.

8 Vail, 1:59. The Walter Perkins map of Pomfret in 1915 appearing in Vail shows original proprietors lots, roads, original farms, and present occupants.

9 PLR, 13:199; 15:296-297, 305; 16:109, 348-349; 17:9.

10 Ibid., 15:603; 17:3, 9, 53, 70, 156; 19:361-362, 472. Hamilton Child, *Gazetteer And Business Directory Of Windsor County, Vermont, For 1883-4* (Syracuse, 1884), 442, hereafter cited as Child.

11 Interview with Walter Howard, 6 February 1986, hereafter cited as Walt Howard. Tucker, 136-137. Child, 442.

12 William H. Dean, "Decay of Rural New England," *The Saturday Review* 70 (October 18, 1890), 454. Amos N. Currier, "The Decline of Rural New England," *Popular Science Monthly* 38 (1891), 384-9.

13 *The Atlantic Monthly* (Boston: Phillips, Sampson And Co, 1857). The title page proclaims the publication "A Magazine Of Literature, Art, And Politics." Ibid., 79 (May 1897), 577-587; 80 (July 1897), 74-83; 83 (April 1899), 561-574.

14 Phillip Morgan, "The Problems Of Rural New England: A Remote Village," *Atlantic Monthly* 79 (May 1897), 577-579.

15 Alvan F. Sanborn, "The Future Of Rural New England," *Atlantic Monthly* 80 (July 1897), 74.

16 Ibid., 76-77, 83.

17 Rollin Lynde Hartt, "A New England Hill Town," *Atlantic Monthly* 83 (April 1899), 563-564.

18 Clarence Deming, "Broken Shadows on the New England Farm," *The Independent* 55 (30 April 1903), 1018-20. William S. Rossiter, "New England's Sick Man – Agriculture," *The Independent* 116 (17 April 1926), 442-443. W. A. Giles, "Is New England Decadent?," *The World Today* 9 (September 1905), 991. Donald Wilhelm, "Is New England Vanishing?," *Colliers Weekly* 74 (11 October 1924), 43. James W. Goldthwait, "A Town That Has Gone Downhill," *Geographical Review* 17 (October, 1927), 527-552.

19 F. Warren Wiggins, "A New Vermont," *The Vermonter* 15, 3 (March 1910), 77-78. Amos Eaton, "Vermont vs. Abandoned Farms," *The Vermonter* 26, 11 (November 1921), 224-226, hereafter cited as Eaton.

20 Bernard DeVoto, "New England, There She Stands," *Harpers Magazine* (March 1932), 405, hereafter cited as DeVoto.

21 Eaton, 224-226.

Chapter 2

1 Barbara Miller Solomon, *Ancestors and Immigrants: A Changing New England Tradition* (Boston: Northeastern University Press, 1956; reprint 1989), 8, 11, 43, 58, 77, 160-161, 167, hereafter cited as Solomon. John M. Lund, "Vermont Nativism: William Paul Dillingham and U.S. Immigration Legislation," *Vermont History* 63 (Winter 1995), 15-18, hereafter cited as Lund. Nancy Gallagher, *Breeding Better Vermonters: The Eugenics Project in the Green Mountain State* (Hanover, N.H.: University Press of New England, 1999), 46, hereafter cited as Gallagher. Wilson, 162.

2 *U.S. Census*, 1870. Hubert Charbonneau et Jacques Legare, *Repertoire des acts de bapteme mariage sepulture et des recensements du Quebec ancien* (Montreal: Universite de Montreal, 1988), 431-432.

3 Interview with Burton Wheeler, 15 July 2001, hereafter cited as Burton Wheeler. Theresa Strouth Gaul, *To Marry an Indian: The Marriage Of Harriett Gold & Elias Boudinot In Letters, 1823-1839* (Chapel Hill: The University of North Carolina Press, 2005), 2-3, 8, 11. Stephen Thernstrom, et al, *Harvard Encyclopedia of American Ethnic Groups* (Cambridge: Harvard University Press, 1980), 391, hereafter cited as Thernstrom. Gerard J. Brault, *The French-Canadian Heritage in New England* (Hanover, N.H.: Univeristy Press of New England, 1986), 52-53, hereafter cited as Brault.

4 Thernstrom, 393. Brault, 54-55.

5 Interview with Albert Dutton, 30 August 2002, hereafter cited as Albert

Dutton. *U.S. Census*, 1880, 1900.

6 *U.S. Census*, 1850, 1860, 1870, 1880, 1900.

7 Wilson, 162.

8 *U.S. Census*, 1870, 1880. Interview with Otis Wheeler, 6 July 1986, hereafter cited as Otis Wheeler.

9 *Pomfret, Vermont Annual Town Report 1889*, 4, hereafter cited *as Pomfret Town Report*.

10 Ibid. *Pomfret, Vermont Town Records*, 1810-1830. F.W. Beers et al, *Atlas of Windsor County, Vermont* (New York: 1869), 17. Vail, 1:122-123, map opposite 332.

11 *U.S. Census*, 1880, 1900.

12 *Pomfret Town Report*, 1890, 2.

13 Ibid., 1891, 2; 1892, 3. U.S. Census, 1900. *Pomfret, Vermont Death Records*, 7:9.

14 *U.S. Census*, 1900, 1910.

15 *Hartford, Vermont Marriage Records*, 3:175. *Hartford, Vermont Birth Records*, 4:42. *Windsor County, Vermont Divorce Records*, 2:649. U.S. Census, 1900. Walt Howard, 17 September 2000.

16 William L. Bowers, *The Country Life Movement in America 1900-1920* (Port Washington, NY: 1974), 4, 16-18, 24, 27. Gallagher, 42-46, 66-78, 95-97, 114-115, 166.

17 Gallagher, 23, 28, 71-75, 78-79, 171-172.

18 Anonymous interview.

19 Gallagher, 131-137, 139, 174-177.

20 Personal experiences of the author. Maude Clifford was the author's grandmother. B.G Jefferis and J.L. Nichols, *Searchlights On Health: the Science of Eugenics* (Naperville, Illinois: J.L. Nichols & Company, 1921).

21 Joe Ranger diary, collection of the author, hereafter cited as JRD. Every extant volume includes entries detailing bestiality. Anonymous interviews.

Chapter 3

1 Otis Wheeler, 6 July 1986. *U.S. Census*, 1900.

2 Interview with Lawrence "Tom" Paronto, 2 October 1998, hereafter cited as Tom Paronto.

3 *PLR*, 21:215. Wilson, 205.

4 Wilson, 98-99, 187-188, 190-191, 204, 208, 214-215, 217, 232, 301, 305-307, 397.

5 Child, 433-445. Includes farmers in Pomfret with mailing addresses for North Pomfret and West Hartford.

6 Ibid. Vail, 2:453, 506-509, 567-569, 582-590, 598-599.

7 Interview with Carlos "Pete" Clifford, 28 October 1992, hereafter cited as Pete Clifford. *Pomfret, Vermont Death Records*, 9/3. *PLR*, 21:217.

8 Constance Strong diary, 2 January; 18 August; 15 October 1915, courtesy of Patricia Birkhead, hereafter cited as CSCD.

9 Ibid., 12, 17-19, 22 Feburary 1916.

10 JRD, January-February; 24 March; 5-7 April; 2-3 May, 9 June; 9 November 1918, 17 January-5 February; 7-19 July 1919.

11 Jane C. Nylander, *Our Own Snug Fireside: Images of the New England Home 1760-1860* (New Haven: Yale University Press, 1993), 200-201. Edwin C. Rozwenc, *Agricultural Policies in Vermont 1860-1945* (Montpelier: Vermont Historical Society, 1981), 120.

12 JRD, 24 February; 14 July; 21 October 1918, 20 January 1919.

13 Wilson, 196-198, 320, 324-325, 335. Rozwenc, 140.

14 Wilson, 336. CSCD, 4, 22 January; 2 July 1915. Edward Clifford diary, 10, 24, 29, 31 May; 5, 12, 17, 19, 24 June 1918, collection of the author, hereafter cited as ECD.

15 JRD. CSCD. ECD. These diaries constantly refer to the daily and seasonal routines of operating a dairy farm.

16 JRD, 1, 4, 18, 21, 28 January; 4, 6, 9, 22, 25, 28 February; 12, 21 March; 1, 8, 10, 22 April; 3, 10, 12, 27 May; 2, 19, 21 June; 12, 31 July; 26 August; 23 September; 21 October; 1 November; 16, 19 December 1918.

17 Ibid., 2, 20 January; 20, 27 February; 3, 20, 27 March; 21 April; 12, 19 May; 12, 20, 30 June; 21 July; 22, 25 August; 22 September; 6, 20 October; 10, 20 November; 1, 22 December 1919.

18 Thomas C. Hubka, "Farm Family Mutuality: The Mid-Nineteenth-

Century Maine Farm Neighborhood," *The Dublin Seminar for New England Folklife Annual Proceedings 1986*, (Boston: Boston University, 1988), 12-23. JRD, 25 January; 30 March; 13 April; 15 August 1920.

19 JRD, 22 April; 3, 23 May 1920.

20 Ibid., 16 January 1918, 24 February 1920.

21 Ibid., 19 January 1918, 24-26, 28-30 June; 1-4, 16, 19-20, 22-23 September 1920. CSCD. ECD, 1918, 1919, 1921.

22 JRD, 1918, 1921, 1937-1939, 1942-1944.

23 Ibid., 22-25 January 1918.

24 Ibid., 26 January-13 March 1918.

25 Ibid., 24-25, 28-30 March; 2, 4, 6-7, 9, 13-14, 16 April 1918.

26 Ibid., 7-15 July 1919.

27 Ibid., 15-30 July 1919.

28 Ibid., 3, 6-8, 10, 14, 17, 20-21, 24, 31 January; 6, 21, 28 February; 1, 3-4, 11, 26-27, 29 March; 28-31 July; 2-9 August 1920.

29 Ibid., 29 August; 1-4, 8-9, 11, 14, 16, 19-20, 22-23 September 1920.

30 Ibid., 4-11 January; 27, 29-30 August; 2, 3, 5-6, 8, 14-17, 19-20 September 1921.

31 Idid., 5 June 1918, 31 May; 11 June; 31 July; 1 August; 2 September; 24 November 1919, 6, 24, 27-28 January; 24 February; 1, 22 June 1920.

Chapter 4

1 Burton Wheeler, 17 July 2001.

2 Walt Howard, 17 September 2000.

3 JRD, 23, 25, 31 January; 18 February 1919.

4 *Pomfret Town Report*, 1919, 6.

5 Wilson, 354-355.

6 JRD, 24 February 1920.

7 Ibid., 26 February 1920.

8 Andrew E. Nuquist, *Town Government In Vermont* (Burlington: University of Vermont, 1964), 94-95.

9 JRD, 20 January; 29 February; 5, 31 March 1920.

10 Ibid., 5, 9, 16 April 1920.

11 Ibid., 17-19 April 1920.

12 Ibid., 20 April 1920. PLR, 22/209.

13 *PLR*, 22:209. JRD, 17 May 1920.

14 JRD, 26, 29 May; 1, 13, 15, 20, 23-26, 28-30 June; 1-3, 17-22, 25 July; 2-9 August; 31 October 1920.

15 Ibid., 4 July 1920.

16 Ibid., 21 April 1921.

17 Loren Pierce to Joe Ranger, 19 May 1921.

18 JRD, 7-8, 10-11 July 1921.

19 Ibid., 2, 9-11, 15-16 August; 8-11 September 1921.

20 Ibid., 24-25 November 1921. *PLR*, 22:352.

21 Burton Wheeler, 15 July 2001. Walt Howard, 17 September 2000. Interview with Charlotte Harvey, 12 January 2003, hereafter cited as Charlotte Harvey. *Vermont Standard*, 21 March 1936. *Pomfret, Vermont Death Records*, 14:8.

22 Wilson, 263-265, 318, 325-326. CSCD 5 April 1928. *Vermont Standard*, 12 April 1923; 27 May; 17, 24 June; 1 July; 25 November 1926, 6 January; 7 April; 16 June 1927.

23 CSCD, 12, 14-15, 17, 19, 26 January; 12, 17, 22, 29 February; 5, 7-8, 18 March; 7 April 1928.

24 Ibid., 12, 26-31 January; 2 February; 1, 5, 8, 12, 16 March; 21, 26, 29 April; 7 May; 6 June 1928.

25 Mary Warren Diary, 10, 20, 26, 30 November; 6, 20, 27 December 1930, courtesy of Charlotte Harvey. Memoranda for November.

26 Ibid., 26 May; 27 October 1931, 13 June; 7, 19 July; 2, 7 August 1934.

27 There is no reference to the creamery or milk cans or milk trucks in Joe Ranger's 1937 diary.

28 *Vermont Standard*, 7 January 1915, 21 June 1917, 16 January; 19 September 1918; 3 April; 23 October 1919, 15, 20, 22 January; 29 April; 2 June; 4 August 1921, 21 June; 25 October; 1 November 1923, 24 April 1924, 27 May; 3, 17,

24 June; 1 July; 25 November 1926, 7 April; 16 June 1927, 16 February 1928.

29 Walt Howard, 17 September 2000. Erwin Clifford, 4 July 2001. Tom Paronto, 2 October 1998.

Chapter 5

1 Interview with Harold "Ted" Paronto, 2 October 1998, hereafter cited as Ted Paronto.

2 Tom Paronto, 2 October 1998.

3 Ibid.

4 Otis Wheeler, 21 December 1990.

5 JRD, 9, 13, 23 May; 5, 13, 27 June; 10 October 1937, 4 March; 24 April; 21, 23 May; 12 June; 31 July; 28, 30 October; 24 November; 10 December 1938, 18 April; 26 September; 30 October; 5, 16 November 1939.

6 Ibid., 21, 23 May 1938; 30 May 1950.

7 Ibid., 31 July; 30 October 1938, 20 December 1942, 29 July; 5 September 1943. Interview with Burton "Slim" King 14 July 1996, hereafter cited as Slim King.

8 JRD, 12 June; 31 July 1938, 30 October 1939, 2 March; 3, 11 April; 11 July; 17 October 1943.

9 Ibid., 6, 10-11 December 1938, 17 December 1939, 10, 31 October; 21 November; 18, 20 December 1942.

10 Ibid., 5, 23 June 1949, 17, 21 May; 15 June; 11 September 1950.

11 Ibid., 4-11 January; 27, 29-30 August; 2-3, 5-6, 8, 14-17, 19-20 September. Otis Wheeler, 6 July 1986. Interview with Alvina Harrington, 5 August 2001, hereafter cited as Alvina Harrington. Interview with John Pitkin and Grace Ballou, 15 August 2002.

12 *PLR*, 19:363; 21:415; 24:143, 186, 225. Ted Paronto, 2 October 1998. JRD, 5 July-4 August 1937.

13 JRD, 4-5, 8-9, 11 January; 12-13, 16-20, 24, 25 February; 24 March; 21, 23-24, 26, 29-30 April; 10-12, 14, 21, 24-26, 29 May; 26, 29-30 June; 2, 5-10, 14, 16, 19-24, 27-30 July; 2, 4 August; 1-11, 14-15, 29-30 September; 1, 4-7, 9, 11, 25, 30 October; 1-4, 6, 8-13, 15-16, 18-19, 23-27 November; 6, 8-10, 13-15, 17, 22 December 1937.

14 Ibid, 10, 12-14 January; 8-9, 14-15, 18 February; 5, 7, 21, 23-26, 28, 29

March; 19 April; 25-26, 28, 30 July; 2-6, 10, 22-23, 26-27, 29-31 August; 6, 8-10, 12-14, 16-17, 22, 25-28, 30 September; 1, 3-4 October; 12, 23, 30 November; 1-3, 7-8, 14-16, 18-22, 24, 31 December 1938.

15 Ibid., 13-16, 18-19, 29-30 September; 2-7, 9-14, 20-23, 25 October; 8-10, 14-18, 20, 22-25, 27 November; 1, 6-7, 13-16, 21-23 December 1939.

16 Ibid., 18-19, 21-24, 29, 30 September; 1-3, 5, 6-10, 29-31 October; 2-4, 6-7, 9, 11, 16, 20, 23 November; 1, 4-5 December 1942.

17 Ibid., 18-22, 27 February; 1, 5, 12-13, 22-26 March; 14-22 September, 4-14 October 1943.

18 Ibid., 3-4, 11-12, 18, 20, 25, 28-29 January; 3-5, 7, 11, 21 February; 21-22, 24 March 1944.

19 Ibid., 8-10, 12 July 1919, 1, 7 April; 23 June 1937, 11 July; 11 November 1938, 29 October 1939, 17 January 1943.

20 Ibid., 11-15 August 1937.

21 Ibid., 16 August 1938.

22 Ibid., 24-27, 30-31 August; 1 September 1943.

23 Ibid., 13, 18-19 January 1937, 16 April 1938.

24 Ibid., 1, 7 April; 23 June; 11-15 August; 30-31 December 1937, 22 January; 4-5, 20-11 February; 16, 18-19 March; 27 April 1938, 27 October; 11 November 1939, 6 August 1942.

25 Ibid., 1 July 1938.

26 Ibid., 11 March 1937.

27 Ibid., 17, 19 June; 12 August 1939.

28 Tom Paronto, 2 October 1998.

29 JRD, 28-30 June; 3, 5-6, 8, 11-12, 14, 16-17 July; 8, 12-23, 26-27, 29-31 August 1938.

30 Tom Paronto, 2 October 1998.

31 Ibid. Interview with Damon Jillson, 28 July 2001, hereafter cited as Damon Jillson.

32 JRD, 23 May; 22 August 1957.

33 Ibid., 14-16, April; 5 May-21 October 1958.

34 Ibid., 7, 17 May; 14, 26-27 August 1958.

35 Ibid., 16 February; 24-25 March; 19 May 1959.

36 Ibid., 16 February; 24-25 March; 22 April-30 November 1959.

37 Ibid., 8 March; 6-17 May 1960. Joe Ranger Check Register, 1963, 1964.

38 *PLR*, 27:176.

39 JRD, 19 February; 25 April 1949.

40 JRD, 26 April; 1, 4, 8, 10, 16, 25 May; 29 August; 10, 25 September 1949.

41 Ibid., 18 October 1949.

42 *Pomfret Town Report*, 1954, 29-32.

43 JRD, 5, 23 June 1949.

Chapter 6

1 *Harvests For Tomorrow* (United States Department of Agriculture Film, 1940), script.

2 Ibid. *Landmark*, 7 August 1941. Interview with Erwin Clifford, 4 July 2001, hereafter cited as Erwin Clifford. Albert Dutton, 30 August 2002.

3 Otis Wheeler, 6 July 1986; 13 August 1989; 1 December 1990. Walt Howard, 17 September 2000.

4 Burton Wheeler, 15 July 2001.

5 Walt Howard, 17 September 2000. Howard's first wife recounted to him Mary Ranger in Lebanon.

6 Interview with Clifford Guthrie, 21 July 2001, hereafter cited as Clifford Guthrie. Interview with Dennis Clay, 14 July 2001, hereafter cited as Dennis Clay. JRD, 22, 29 July; 5 August; 12 September; 28 October 1942.

7 Tom Paronto, 2 October 1998.

8 Ted Paronto, 2 October 1998. Alvina Harrington, 5 August 2001. Erwin Clifford, 4 July 2001. Dennis Clay 24 July 2001. Interview with Irene Brockway, 1 July 2001, hereafter cited as Irene Brockway. Interview with Henry Small, 11 July 2001, hereafter cited as Henry Small.

9 Tom Paronto, 2 October 1998.

10 Interview with Scott Harrington, 12 July 2001, hereafter cited as Scott Harrington.

11 Pete Clifford, 6 July 2001.

12 Burton Wheeler, 15 July 2001.

13 Henry Small, 11 July 2001.

14 Erwin Clifford, 4 July 2001.

15 Scott Harrington, 12 July 2001. Tom Paronto, 2 October 1998.

16 Tom Paronto, 2 October 1998. Walt Howard, 17 September 2000.

17 Erwin Clifford, 4 July 2001. Walt Howard, 17 September 2000. Tom Paronto, 2 October 1998. Ted Paronto, 2 October 1998.

18 Conversation with Carolyn Toby.

19 Erwin Clifford, 4 July 2001.

20 Ibid. Dennis Clay, 14 July 2001. Damon Jillson, 28 July 2001. Irene Brockway, 1 July 2001.

21 Erwin Clifford, 4 July 2001. Dennis Clay, 14 July 2001.

22 Irene Brockway, 1 July 2001. Alvina Harrington, 5 August 2001.

23 Scott Harrington, 14 July 2001.

24 Alvina Harrington, 5 August 2001.

25 Albert Dutton, 30 August 2002. Clifford Guthrie, 21 July 2001.

26 Erwin Clifford, 4 July 2001.

27 Dennis Clay, 14 July 2001.

28 Ibid.

29 Scott Harrington, 14 July 2001.

30 Slim King, 14 July 1996.

31 Ibid.

32 Tom Paronto, 2 October 1998.

33 Ibid. Ted Paronto, 2 October 1998.

34 Walt Howard, 17 September 2000.

35 Ted Paronto, 2 October 1998. Erwin Clifford, 4 July 2001.

36 Burton Wheeler, 15 July 2001. Pete Clifford, 6 July 2001.

37 Pete Clifford, 6 July 2001. Irene Brockway, 1 July 2001.

38 Interview with Lois Brockway, 13 January 2003, hereafter cited as Lois Brockway.

39 Henry Small, 11 July 2001.

40 Zadock Thompson, *History Of Vermont, Natural, Civil, And Statistical* (Burlingon: Chauncey Goodrich, 1842), 39. Tom Paronto, 2 October 1998.

41 Dennis Clay, 14 July 2001.

42 Vermont Standard, 23 July 1953. OWD, 1 February 1961. Scott Harrington, 12 July 2001. Burton Wheeler, 15 July 2001. Tom Paronto, 2 October 1998. Erwin Clifford, 4 July 2001. Clifford Guthrie, 21 July 2001. Dennis Clay, 14 July 2001. Irene Brockway, 1 July 2001.

43 Private conversation.

44 Erwin Clifford, 4 July 2001.

45 Pete Clifford, 6 July 2001.

46 JRD, 24 October 1919, 28 October; 2, 3 November 1939, 30 October 1943. APD, 14 October 1952. Alvina Harrington, 5 August 2001. Ted Paronto, 2 October 1998.

47 Private conversation.

48 Walt Howard, 17 September 2000. Tom Paronto, 2 October 1998.

49 Ted Paronto, 2 October 1998.

50 Tom Paronto, 2 October 1998.

51 Slim King, 14 July 1996.

52 Irene Brockway, 1 July 2001.

53 Interview with Melvin Young, 17 August 2002. Interview with Richard Brockway, 13 January 2003, hereafter cited as Richard Brockway.

54 Walt Howard, 17 September 2000, 11 June 2004.

55 Damon Jillson, 28 July 2001.

56 Ibid.

57 Richard Brockway, 13 January 2003. Lois Brockway, 13 January 2003.

58 Irene Brockway, 1 July 2001.

Chapter 7

1 Andrea Rebeck, "The Selling of Vermont: From Agriculture to Tourism, 1860-1910," *Vermont History* 44 (Winter 1976), 22-27.

2 Ibid. *Homeseeker's Guide To Vermont Farms*, Guy W. Bailey, Secretary of State, Vermont Publicity Department, Orlando L. Martin Commissioner of Agriculture (St. Albans, Vermont: 1911). *Vermont Farms: Some Facts and Figures Concerning the Agricultural Resources and Opportunities of the Green Mountain State*, Vermont Bureau of Publicity (Essex Jct., Vermont: [1913]). *Vermont Farms And Summer Homes For Sale 1927*, Vermont Bureau of Publicity (Montpelier, Vermont: 1927).

3 *Vermont Summer Homes*, Dorothy Canfield, Vermont Bureau of Publicity (Montpelier, Vermont: 1934), [1]. *Vermont Life.*

4 Henry Swan Dana, *History of Woodstock, Vermont* (Boston and New York: Houghton, Mifflin and Company, 1889; reprint, Woodstock, Vermont: 1980), 231-275, 328-348, 453-489. Peter Jennison, *History of Woodstock, Vermont 1890-1983* (Woodstock, Vermont: The Woodstock Foundation, 1985), 185-253.

5 *Map, Roads And Summer Homes: Woodstock, Vermont 1934*, A.S. Buel. *Roads and Country Homes near Woodstock, Vermont 1949*, Alice Standish Buel. *Map, Roads and Country Homes near Woodstock, Vermont 1965*, Douglas Ross.

6 This analysis is based on the history of the surviving seventy-eight out of the ninety-two houses shown in the North Pomfret area on Walter Perkins' 1915 map of Pomfret. Deed research shows that sixty-one of the seventy-eight houses surviving (or new houses having been replaced on the same foundation by the gentrifiers) in 1990 were gentrified as follows by decade: 1920s, 4; 1930s, 10; 1940s, 11; 1950s, 7; 1960s, 19; 1970s, 6; 1980's, 4.

7 John Gould, *New England Town Meeting: Safeguard of Democracy* (Brattleboro, Vermont: Stephen Day Press, 1940). DeVoto, 405-415.

8 DeVoto, 407.

9 Ibid., 407-408.

10 Ibid., 408.

11 Ibid., 408-409.

12 Ibid., 409, 415.

13 Margaret and Walter Hard, *This is Vermont* (Brattleboro, Vermont Stephen Daye Press: 1936), hereafter cited as Hard.

14 *Automobile Tours From Woodstock Inn* (Woodstock, Vermont: Elm Tree Press, 1915). *The Jarvis Auto Tours: Sight-Seeing Journeys To Historic And Picturesque Places In Vermont* (Burlington, Vermont: Hays Advertising Agency, 1915[?]). Hard, 1-2, 12-13, 65, 71-72, 100-107, 114-115, 118-119, 141, 146, 149, 181, 184, 197, 213, 215, 219, 223, 230, 245, 249-250, 253.

15 Hard, 71, 100-107.

16 Ibid., 213, 215.

17 Ibid., 219.

18 Henry Lent, *Sixty Acres More or Less* (New York: The MacMillan Company, 1941), 1-2, hereafter cited as Lent.

19 Ibid., 19-20.

20 Ibid., 20-21.

21 Ibid., 21-24.

22 Elliott Merrick, *Green Mountain Farm* (New York: The MacMillan Company, 1948; second edition, 1949), dust jacket, hereafter cited as Merrick.

23 Ibid., 1, 6-9, 39.

24 Ibid., 10.

25 Ibid., 22.

26 Ibid., 22-23.

27 Ibid., 23.

28 Ibid., 39, 67.

29 Ibid., 40-41.

30 Ibid., 51.

31 Elsie and John Masterson, *Nothing Whatever To Do* (New York: Crown Publishers, 1956), hereafter cited as Masterson.

32 Ibid., 65-66, 95.

33 Ibid., 99.

34 Ibid., 94-95.

35 Ibid., 21, 67, 94.

36 Ibid., 110-112.

37 Ibid., 113.

38 Judd Hale, *The Education Of A Yankee* (New York: Harper & Row, 1987), 208-209.

39 Edward Connery Latham, "The Gentle Jesters," *Yankee* (January 1957), 30-33, 78.

40 Allen R. Foley Papers, Rauner Special Collections Library, Dartmouth College Library, 2 Boxes, hereafter cited as Foley Papers.

41 Ibid. Allen R. Foley, *What the Old-Timer Said* (Brattleboro, Vermont: The Stephen Greene Press, 1971), hereafter cited as *Old-Timer*.

42 Foley Papers. *Old-Timer*, 5.

43 Foley Papers.

44 Foley Papers. Allen R. Foley, *The Old-Timer Talks Back* (Brattleboro, Vermont: The Stephen Greene Press, 1975).

45 *Old-Timer*, 1-12, 24-25, 32-33.

46 Orris Bushway to Lyman Herriman, 22 May; 26 June 1934. *Vermont Standard*, 12 May 1932, 9 March; 11 May; 14 September 1944, 5 July; 18 October; 1 November 1945.

47 Charlotte Harvey, 12 January 2003.

Chapter 8

1 Private Conversation.

2 Lent, passim. Merrick, passim. Masterson, passim.

3 Interview with Andy Marshall, 25 February 1994, hereafter cited as Andy Marshall. *PLR*, 24:272.

4 Andy Marshall, 25 February 1994.

5 Ibid.

6 Ibid.

7 *PLR*, 27:157. Interview with Debbie Coogan, 2 September 1992. Interview with Matt Coogan, 14 July 2001. Interview with Rosalind Anderson, 14 July 2001, hereafter cited as Rosalind Anderson. Dennis Clay, 14 July 2001.

8 Rosalind Anderson, 14 July 2001. Dennis Clay, 14 July 2001.

9 Rosalind Anderson, 14 July 2001.

10 Ibid.

11 Ibid.

12 Ibid.

13 Interview with Jane and Will Curtis, 17 February 2003, hereafter cited as Curtis. *Hartford, Vermont Land Records*, 55:310. Will Curtis, *The Second Nature of Things* (Hopewell, N.J.: The Ecco Press, 1992), 230-231, hereafter cited as *Second Nature*.

14 Ibid.

15 Ibid.

16 Curtis, 17 February 2003.

17 Ibid.

Chapter 9

1 Burton Wheeler, 15 July 2001.

2 Photographs courtesy of Damon Jillson, Betty Cross, Charlotte Harvey, Bill Burch, Wayne Thompson, Collamer Abbott, Hanson Carroll. *Grit*, 2 August 1977. *Valley News*, 7 January 1957. *Vermont Standard*, 1 January 1987.

3 Ibid.

4 Burton Wheeler, 15 July 2001.   Damon Jillson, 28 July 2001.   Clifford Guthrie, 21 July 2001.

5 Photo courtesy of Damon Jillson.

6 Clifford Guthrie, 21 July 2001. Leslie Hazen was Guthrie's wife's cousin.

7 Interview with Wayne Thompson, 28 March 2003.

8 Ibid.

9 Interview with Collamer Abbott, 16, 19, 31 August; 23 November 2002, hereafter cited as Abbott.

10 Ibid.

11 Ibid. *Valley News*, 9 June 2002, supplement "50 Years Of The Valley News." *Dartmouth Alumni Directory* (Hanover N.H.: Dartmouth Publications, 1961), 233, 288.

12 Collamer Abbott, 16, 19, 31 August; 23 November 2002.

13 Ibid.

14 Ibid.

15 Interview with Hanson Carroll, 29 January 2003, hereafter cited as Hanson Carroll. *Vermont Life.* Carroll has 40 *Vermont Life* front and back cover photographs. Interview with George Mitchell, 29 July 2005. Collamer Abbott, 16 May 2003.

16 Hanson Carroll, 29 January 2003. *Vermont Life,* covers for Summer 1970 and Fall 1972.

17 *Valley News,* 7 January 1957.

18 Ibid.

19 Ibid.

20 Ibid.

21 JRD, 5, 12 October 1957, 13 October 1958, 19, 21 July; 2 August; 26 September 1954.

22 Hanson Carroll, "Order and Disorder," *Yankee* (January 1962), 28-29.

23 Ibid.

Chapter 10

1 Scott Harrington, 12 July 2001.

2 Ibid.

3 Ibid.

4 *Pomfret Town Report,* 1954, 15-23; 1955, 15-21; 1956, 17-23; 1957, 20-27.

5 Ibid., 1959, 5; 1960, 7.

6 Ibid., 1957, 5.

7 Scott Harrington, 12 July 2001.

8 *Vermont Standard,* 13 February; 14 August 1958. *Pomfret Town Report,* 1958, 30. Erwin Clifford, 4 July 2001. Pete Clifford, 6 July 2001.

9 JRD, 1, 3 December 1959.

10 Ibid., 1958.

11 Courtesy of Albert Dutton. JRD, 1 December 1959.

12 JRD, 5, 9, 10-11, 14, 20 December 1958.

13 Ibid., 28 January; 8 March; 12 April 1959.

14 *Pomfret Town Report*, 1955, 2; 1956, 2; 1957, 2; 1958, 2; 1959, 1; 1960, 3; 1961, 3. Albert Parker diary, 23 January 1949, 16 October 1960, courtesy of Louise Silloway, hereafter cited as APD.

15 APD, 25 October; 20, 29 November 1960.

16 Ibid., 10, 18, 30 December 1960.

17 Private conversation. APD, 11, 13, 31 January; 1, 13, 21 February 1961.

18 APD, 25 February; 8, 19, 30 March; 15 April 1961.

19 Ibid., 12 August; 22 October 1961.

20 *Pomfret Town Report*, 1952, 2; 1953, 2; 1954, 2; 1955, 2; 1956, 2; 1957, 2; 1958, 2; 1959, 1; 1960, 3.

21 Otis Wheeler diary, 2, 5 January 1939, courtesy of Hertha Wheeler, hereafter cited as OWD.

22 Ibid., 31 January; 4, 5, 6, 14, 20 May; 29 June; 1, 8, 9 July 1949.

23 Ibid., 1, 19 February; 6, 15, 20 April; 16 July; 3, 17, 19 December 1961.

24 Ibid., 11, 14, 27 January; 4, 8, 18, 25 February; 2, 23 March; 8, 14, 20-21, 27 April; 5 May; 7-8, 14-17, 21-22, 24-25, 28 June; 15, 17, 21, 27 July; 3-6, 10, 19, 31 August; 28-30 September; 12, 17, 27 October; 3, 17, 22 November; 2, 7, 8, 21-23, 25, 28 December 1962.

25 Ibid., 21 June; 21 July 1962, 18-19 July; 9 September; 31 October; 1 December 1964. Henry Small, 11 July 2001.

26 OWD, 14-17, 21-22, 24 June 1962.

27 Ibid., 25, 28 June; 15, 17 July 1962.

28 Ibid., 21, 27 July; 3-6, 10, 19 August; 28, 30 September 1962.

29 Ibid., 19 May; 6 June; 6, 10-11, 20 August; 10 October 1963, 21-22, 27 May; 3-4, 14, 20 July; 14, 20 August; 1, 4-6 September 1964.

30 Ibid., 17 October 1962, 2 November 1963, 5 November 1964.

31 Ibid., 22 November; 23, 25 December 1962, 28 November; 25 December 1963.

32 Ibid., 5 May; 26-27 December 1963, 8-9, 11 November 1964.

33 Henry Small, 11 July 2001.

34 *Pomfret, Vermont Death Records*, 15:143. OWD, 1, 5, 21 October; 2, 5, 8-9, 11-12, 14, 26-27 November; 1 December 1964.

35 Scott Harrington, 12 July 2001.

36 Ibid. APD, 1 December 1964. OWD, 1, 2 December 1964. Burton Wheeler, 15 July 2001.

Chapter 11

1 *Vermont Standard*, 10 December 1964.

2 *Associated Press*, 28 July 1977, hereafter cited as Shulins.

3 Ibid.

4 Ibid.

5 Ibid.

6 Ibid. Private Conversation. Scott Harrington, 12 July 2001.

7 Shulins.

8 Ibid.

9 Albert Dutton, 30 August 2002. Burton Wheeler, 15 July 2001. Walt Howard, 17 September 2000. Interview with Josephine Dupuis, 15 August 2003, hereafter cited as Josephine Dupuis.

10 Henry Small, 11 July 2001. Tom Paronto, 2 October 1998. Damon Jillson, 28 July 2001.

11 Interview with Carl Johnson, 10 August 2001, hereafter cited as Carl Johnson.

12 OWD, 9 December 1965.

13 Carl Johnson, 10 August 2001.

14 Ibid. Conversation with Pat Stark.

15 Ibid.

16 Carl Johnson, 10 August 2001.

Chapter 12

1 *Pomfret Town Report*, 1964, 32. *PLR*, 22/352.

2 *PLR*, 27:176. Windsor County Probate Records, hereafter cited as WCPR.

3 Interview with Walter and Edith Pyle, 23 March 2002.

4 Walt Howard, 17 February 2003.

5 *PLR*, 29:173-174. WCPR. Vermont Agency of Natural Resources, Department of Forests, Parks & Recreation, Waterbury, Vermont, file, hereafter cited as VANR.

6 Interview with Robert Caposella, 29 June 2002. Private conversation.

7 Personal observation of the author.

8 VANR.

9 Ibid. Walt Howard, 17 September 2000.

10 *PLR*, 30:28. Walt Howard, 17 September 2000.

11 This analysis is based on the history of the surviving seventy-eight out of the ninety-two houses shown in the North Pomfret area on Walter Perkins' 1915 map of Pomfret. Deed research shows that sixty-one of the seventy-eight houses surviving (or new houses having been replaced on the same foundation by the gentrifiers) in 1990 were gentrified as follows by decade: 1920s, 4; 1930s, 10; 1940s, 11; 1950s, 7; 1960s, 19; 1970s, 6; 1980's, 4. *Map, Roads And Summer Homes: Woodstock, Vermont 1934*, A.S. Buel. *Roads and Country Homes near Woodstock, Vermont 1949*, Alice Standish Buel. *Map, Roads and Country Homes near Woodstock, Vermont 1965*, Douglas Ross.

12 *Valley News*, 20 June; 17, 22 July; 5, 6 September 1969.

13 Interview with John Anderson, 5 March 2004, hereafter cited as John Anderson. Andy Marshall, 25 February 1994. Interview with Orson St. John. *Pomfret Post*, 1, 2 (September 1971). Interview with Peter and Daphne Gratiot. Private conversations. *Pomfret Post*, Vol. 1, No. 2 (September 1971). *Vermont Standard*, 6 January; 23 March; 30 March; 25 May 1972.

14 *Quechee Times*, December 1977-January 1978.

15 Pomfret Associates: Design Goals And Lot Narratives, January 1981, Pomfret, Vermont Town Clerk's Office. *Valley News*, 7 February 1987, 25 May 1990. *Appeal By the Town Of Pomfret Of The Redetermination Of The 1991 Equalized Education Property Value*, 7 April 2000, Pomfret Town Clerk's Office. Andy Marshall, 25 February 1994. John Anderson, 5 March 2004. *Vermont*

Standard, 1 January 1987. *Green Mountain Gazzette*, July 1990. *Second Nature*, 230-231.

16 Shulins, *Vermont Standard*, 1 January 1987.

17 *Valley News*, 7 February 1987.

18 Ibid., 25 May 1990.

19 Ibid.

20 Curtis, 17 February 2003.

21 *Second Nature*, 230-231.

22 Ibid.

23 Ibid.

24 Copy of original story sent to Janice Aitken, courtesy of Collamer Abbott. *Green Mountain Gazette*, July 1990.

25 Ibid.

26 Ibid.

Index